CUTTING EDGE

THIRD EDITION

UPPER INTERMEDIATE

WORKBOOK

WITH KEY

**JANE COMYNS CARR FRANCES EALES
AND DAMIAN WILLIAMS**

CONTENTS

Language focus 1
Past and present verb forms

1a Match sentence beginnings A with endings B.

A
1 Vicki's a marketing manager, and
2 When I got home last night
3 Ben *was feeling* sorry for himself because
4 My sister's *trying* to
5 I *haven't been* to a football match for ages,
6 They've *been* in this class
7 I'm *thinking about* studying
8 When I was young, Dad *used to do* the shopping

B
a he'*d just split up* with his girlfriend.
b abroad next year.
c she spends a lot of time *sitting* in meetings.
d since last term.
e and Mum did the cooking.
f not since England beat Germany.
g my flatmate *had cooked* me dinner!
h learn Greek at the moment.

b Complete the sentences so they are true for you.

1 I'm a _____ and I spend a lot of time _____ .
2 When I got home last night _____ .
3 This time last year / month / week, I was feeling _____ because I'd/I hadn't _____ .
4 At the moment, I'm _____ .
5 I haven't _____ for a long time.
6 I've _____ since _____ .
7 I'm thinking about _____ .
8 When I was young, _____ .

2 Write complete sentences, using the correct Present simple or continuous form and making any other necessary changes.

1 I / organise / a party for Clare's birthday. Who / you / think / I should invite?
I'm organising a party for Clare's birthday. Who do you think I should invite?

2 What / you / cook? It / smell / wonderful!
_____

3 A lot of / people / believe / he / be / very talented but / I / not agree.
_____

4 A: Why / you / be / so friendly today?
_____
B: I / be / just / in a good mood!
_____

5 You / know / Ken? He / be / very interesting. He / work / at the Science Museum.
_____

6 I / read / this great book. It / be / about growing up during the 1960s.
_____

3 In this extract from a soap opera script, complete the gaps with the Past simple or Past continuous form of the verbs in the box.

come	happen	just discuss	just try
not tell	stop	~~talk~~	think

Duncan and Tessa are talking. Carla comes in and Duncan and Tessa immediately stop. They look guilty. Duncan gets up to go.

Duncan: Hi, Carla. Is that the time? I've got to go. Bye.

Carla: Bye. (looks suspiciously at Tessa) Hi, Tessa. What ¹*were you talking* about when I ²_____ in?

Tessa: Oh, nothing!

Carla: Then why ³_____ ? Come on, tell me.

Tessa: OK. We ⁴_____ Graham's new girlfriend.

Carla: (sitting down suddenly) New girlfriend? When ⁵_____ this _____ ?

Tessa: A few weeks ago.

Carla: Why ⁶_____ me?

Tessa: We ⁷_____ you'd be upset. We ⁸_____ to spare your feelings.

Carla: You'd better tell me all about it.

Tessa: OK. Look, would you like a drink first?

4 Tick the correct ending.

1 I've been to the Pompidou Centre twice
   a while I was in Paris.
   b so I don't really want to go there again. ✓

2 Denise and Adam have been married for five years
   a and they were very happy.
   b and they're very happy.

3 I lost my car keys –
   a I can't find them anywhere.
   b I couldn't find them anywhere.

4 How long have you lived on your own
   a in this flat?
   b before you met Lisa?

5 Steve's been very depressed
   a last week.
   b all week.

6 John worked for the company for ten years
   a and we're sorry that he's leaving.
   b and we were sorry when he left.

5 Circle the correct verb form.

1 The teacher *wasn't believing* / *didn't believe*
   Jack's story about the dog eating his homework.

2 *Can you smell* / *Are you smelling* burning?

3 I *don't remember* / *'m not remembering* where I
   met Hassan.

4 I love this colour. What *are you thinking* / *do you
   think*?

5 Shona *isn't owning* / *doesn't own* her flat, she
   rents it.

6 Can I call you back later? I*'m having* / *have* an
   English lesson at the moment.

7 What's that noise coming from downstairs?
   Something *is seeming* / *seems* strange to me.

8 I *don't like* / *'m not liking* the way they're looking
   at us.

**6 Correct the mistakes. There is one mistake in each
sentence.**

     started
1 Liam ~~used to start~~ his first job when he was 18.

2 I used to be late for work twice last week.

3 Chloe didn't used to be afraid of flying, but she is
   now.

4 I used to be hating broccoli when I was little, but
   now I love it!

5 What's happened to Ben and Mila? They've never
   used to fight like that.

6 What games used you to play when you were
   younger?

7 Last weekend I used to go out with my friends.

8 Before I moved here, I had used to live in Ohio.

**7 Complete the sentences with the Past simple or Past
perfect form of the verb in brackets.**

1 Paul failed his driving test because he *hadn't
   practised* (practise) enough.

2 When Jess _____ (see) the car, she couldn't believe
   Alex had paid so much for it.

3 I was feeling a bit upset because I _____ (hear)
   some bad news about my brother.

4 By the time he was 13, Mozart _____ (write) many
   symphonies.

5 I hadn't revised for the exam, so I _____ (not
   know) what to write.

6 Mrs Reynolds _____ (forget) to lock the door and
   when she came back her house had been burgled.

7 I thought I _____ (leave) the report on my desk,
   but I couldn't find it anywhere.

8 When Pierre started watching the film, he realised
   he _____ (already see) it.

**8 Complete the gaps with the correct form of the verb
in brackets.**

Child prodigy

Eleven-year-old Nigel Matsuchek ¹*has become* (become)
the youngest person ever to be accepted at Oxford
University. He ²_____ (celebrate) with his family
yesterday after he ³_____ (get) a letter offering
him a place to study physics. 'When he heard the post
arrive, he ⁴_____ (go) to check it,' explained his
mother, 'and when we heard him shout "Yes!" we knew
he ⁵_____ (receive) the news he wanted. He ⁶
_____ (work) so hard over the last few years and
it's what he really wants to do. We ⁷_____ (be) so
proud of him.'

Jackie Lane:
Live Tonight!

'My next guest ⁸_____
(never have) any problems with
getting what he wanted. When
he first came to the United States
he ⁹_____ (not have) any
money and he ¹⁰_____
(work) in a factory during the day and at a nightclub at
night to support his family. Now he ¹¹_____
(become) one of the richest people in the world.
Between 1997 and 2004, while he ¹²_____ (live)
in Florida, he ¹³_____ (manage) two hugely
successful e-businesses and he ¹⁴_____ (just
write) a best-selling book: *Ten Steps to Success*. This
week, he ¹⁵_____ (visit) his business school in
Chicago and tonight he ¹⁶_____ (spend) an
evening with us. Ladies and gentlemen, please welcome
Simon Bach!

Listen and read
A date with disaster?

9a 🎧 **1.1** Listen to and/or read the stories and decide who had the worst experience.

b Listen and/or read again and choose the correct name: Celine, Rodrigo, Robert or Claire.

1 Who had a date by the sea?
   Celine and Rodrigo

2 Who had known the other person for some time before the date?
   _____

3 Who wanted to impress the person they dated?
   _____

4 Who was much older than the person they dated?
   _____

5 Who had an accident?
   _____

6 Who was embarrassed by the other person's behaviour?
   _____

7 Whose date was very expensive?
   _____

8 Who went out with the person again?
   _____

Vocabulary
Relationships

10 Choose the correct option to complete each sentence.

1 I've always been very close _____ my sister. We do lots of things together.
   a with   **b** to   **c** of

2 Natalie didn't enjoy her job after she fell _____ with her boss.
   a out   **b** off   **c** on

3 Don't listen to them, they're jealous _____ your success.
   a of   **b** about   **c** from

4 Do you get _____ with your cousins?
   a about   **b** of   **c** on

5 I hate being around Owen and Liz. They're always putting each other _____ .
   a on   **b** down   **c** around

6 Josh had always been loyal _____ his friend, even when other people didn't believe him.
   a to   **b** on   **c** with

7 Will always felt threatened _____ his brother's musical abilities.
   a from   **b** with   **c** by

8 Even as young boys, Mark and Chris would always compete _____ each other.
   a with   **b** at   **c** by

A date with disaster?

Have you ever been on a first date with someone you really liked and found that it turned into a disaster before your very eyes? We interviewed two people who have had just this experience.

Celine, 27, Hairdresser.

Robert Buckley, 24, Fitness Instructor.

Celine: The worst first date I've ever had was while I was on holiday in Majorca. I must have been about eighteen, and I met this gorgeous Spanish waiter, Rodrigo. He was a good ten years older than me and had dark brown eyes and black curly hair. Well, after we'd had a few drinks in a local bar, he suggested going for a romantic walk along the beach. Things seemed to be going quite well, even though we didn't have much in common. Then we walked past a couple of guys who were standing at the water's edge talking. When they looked across at us, Rodrigo stared at them aggressively. He asked them what their problem was, and what they were looking at. They hadn't even being looking at us before that, but he started arguing with them. His behaviour was a real turn-off and made me uncomfortable. I felt so ashamed that I just walked away. I never dated Rodrigo again, as you can imagine.

Robert: She was someone I knew from school and I'd always really fancied her. I had just got a new motorbike, a Suzuki 250, which I was really proud of. So anyway, one Saturday afternoon, I asked her to come out for a ride and we went up to a disused airfield a few kilometres away. There was no one else around, so I started driving with one wheel in the air and going really fast. Claire said she loved it and could she have a go at riding it. I couldn't see why not – but how wrong can you be?

Once she'd managed to start it and stay upright, she suddenly got a bit over-confident and zoomed off at top speed towards some trees. As I started running after her, I could see that she was losing control of the bike, and a minute later – bang! She went straight into a tree. Claire was a bit shocked and bruised, but my beautiful Suzuki was a wreck and cost me a fortune to repair. We did see each other again, but from then on we stuck to public transport.

Vocabulary
Friendship

11 Replace the phrases in bold with the correct form of a word/phrase in the box.

behind her back   confide in   ~~fun to be with~~
gossip   keep his / her / their / your promises
lie   tell the truth   trust

1 You're going to love Christie, she's really **lively and makes you have a good time**. _fun to be with_
2 Don't **say something false** to me, I know where you went last night! _____
3 It felt good knowing he always had someone to **tell his secrets to**. _____
4 I can't **believe in** Emma any more, not after what she did. _____
5 You shouldn't talk about her **without her knowing** like that. She's not here to defend herself. _____
6 Harry felt much better after he'd **said** to his girlfriend **what actually happened**. _____
7 My parents always **did what they said they were going to do** when I was younger. _____
8 You don't know if that's true, it's just **something that may or may not be true**. _____

Language focus 2
Uses of auxiliary verbs

12 Match beginnings A with endings B, then add the auxiliary *do* to give more emphasis.

A
1 Come to the party.   _e_
2 Ben looks well.   ___
3 I hate it.   ___
4 We didn't like the hotel,   ___
5 I like fish generally,   ___

B
a when people are late for meetings.
b but I don't like it raw.
c but we enjoyed the tours.
d Has he been on holiday?
e I'm sure you'll enjoy it.

1 _Do come to the party. I'm sure you'll enjoy it._
2 _____
3 _____
4 _____
5 _____

13 Write questions using an auxiliary verb. Then choose a follow-up phrase from the box.

~~Neither do I.~~   How long has she had it?   I don't.
I hope he enjoys it.   It's OK, I've got some chicken.
Why not?

1 I don't really like jazz.
   Don't you? Neither do I. _____

2 My sister Stefania's got a Yamaha.
   _____
   _____

3 I'm not going to buy that house after all.
   _____
   _____

4 Jack's never been to a football match before.
   _____
   _____

5 I agree with Tim.
   _____
   _____

6 There wasn't any fresh salmon left in the shop.
   _____
   _____

14 Cross out unnecessary words and add auxiliary verbs if necessary to make the conversations more natural.

1 A: Do they accept credit cards on the underground?
   B: Well, yes they ~~accept credit cards on the underground~~, but only for amounts over £10.
   (do)
2 A: The children have been skating before, haven't they?
   B: Well, John has been skating before, but Trevor and Ann haven't been skating before.
3 A: You're not going to leave the company, are you?
   B: Yes, I am going to leave the company, actually.
4 A: Does the flight stop over at Vancouver?
   B: Yes, it stops over at Vancouver for two hours.
5 A: Has the school got a website?
   B: I think it has got a website, but I'll check for you.
6 A: Was it snowing when your plane landed?
   B: No, it wasn't snowing when my plane landed, but it was very cold.

Pronunciation

Stressed and unstressed auxiliary verbs

15a Look at the conversations below and decide if the auxiliary verb underlined is stressed (S) or unstressed (U).

    1 A: How <u>do</u> you feel today?   <u>U</u>
       B: Much better, thanks.

    2 A: <u>Do</u> you love me?   ——
       B: Of course I <u>do</u>.   ——

    3 A: I don't believe it! Chelsea <u>are</u> losing! ——
       B: <u>Are</u> they? I thought they'd win this easily! ——

    4 A: She doesn't like me, <u>does</u> she?   ——
       B: Yes she <u>does</u>, don't be silly.   ——

    5 A: Trudi's not a very good singer.   ——
       B: Yes she <u>is</u>! How can you say that?   ——

    6 A: <u>You're</u> not listening to me, love.   ——
       B: I <u>am</u> listening to you!   ——

  b 🎧 **1.2 Listen and check.**

Wordspot

get

16 Circle the correct form of *get* and complete the gaps with the words in the box.

angry	flight	~~job~~	message		over
presents	tired	work			

    1 I'd like **getting / get /** (**to get**) a better *job* with a higher salary.

    2 I **got / 'm getting / have got** the early _____ from London to New York yesterday.

    3 Sometimes my husband **gets / is getting / was getting** so _____ he can't keep his eyes open.

    4 The children never **get / used to get / are getting** many _____ on their birthdays because we couldn't afford much.

    5 **Do you get / Did you get / Were you getting** the _____ I left on your answerphone?

    6 I **got / was getting / get** to _____ very late this morning, so my boss wasn't pleased.

    7 A: How are you?
       B: Much better, thanks. I think I **got / get / 've got** _____ my cold now.

    8 My brother **had got / was getting / got** _____ when I told him I couldn't help him.

Language live

Responding to how people feel

17a Insert a word from the box into each response below.

a	any	down	how	ignore	matter
~~mind~~	must	no	to	sounds	up

    1 A: I'm sorry! I've spilt my coffee all over your tablecloth.
           mind
       B: Never ^. It's easily washable.

    2 A: I can't stop thinking about Helen's operation.
       B: Try not worry about it. There's nothing you can do.

    3 A: The kids at school keep laughing at my hair.
       B: Don't take notice of them.

    4 A: I think my boss heard me saying that he annoys me.
       B: He probably didn't hear you. There's point in getting upset about it.

    5 A: I've got to have four teeth out tomorrow.
       B: That awful!

    6 A: My son is going into hospital for tests next week.
       B: You be really worried.

    7 A: I can't believe we're not going to have you as our teacher any more.
       B: Cheer! Your new teacher's really nice.

    8 A: I just can't do it! I'm too nervous! Someone else will have to give the speech.
       B: Calm! You'll be fine.

    9 A: Andy said my dress makes me look fat!
       B: Just him. You look perfect!

   10 A: Our car won't be ready until the weekend.
       B: Annoying!

   11 A: I'm so sorry. I completely forgot to bring that book you wanted to borrow.
       B: Don't worry, it doesn't.

   12 A: The date was going really well, until he started telling me about his political views.
       B: What shame! I guess you won't be seeing him again, then.

  b 🎧 **1.3 Listen and check.**

Writing
Planning and drafting a biography

18a Match the beginnings in A with the endings in B to
make phrases from a biography of a novelist.

A

1 Born in
2 As a
3 Later
4 It was while she was working in Dundee
5 Despite the unexpected success of
her first novel,
6 After sending
7 As time passed
8 Now in her sixties, she is still
9 Recently
10 They live in Los Angeles

B

a she became very well-known.
b she accepted an invitation to write a television
series.
c she taught English and ...
d teenager, ...
e as active as ever.
f and have two children.
g this was followed by a period when she
wrote very little.
h her second novel to ten publishers, it was finally
accepted.
i that she met her future husband.
j Chicago in 1949, ...

b Write a biography of the actor, George Clooney
using the notes below. Organise the information and
include some of the phrases from exercise *a*.

- appearance: dark eyes and dark hair with some grey
- looks older than he is, but still very handsome
- 1989-1993 - married to Talia Balsam
- has had many girlfriends in recent years, including Italian
  actress Elisabetta Canalis
- still enjoys a bachelor life with a group of friends who spend
  time at his house, playing basketball, relaxing, etc.
- born in 1961
- grew up in Kentucky. Father was a famous host of a TV
  talk show. George loved being part of a famous family - got
  interested in show business
- 21, drove to Los Angeles - stayed with aunt and did whatever
  jobs he could get
- worked for 13 years in small TV shows then joined the cast of
  ER in 1994 as Doug Ross
- major film roles since ER, including Ocean's Eleven, Up in the
  Air and The Descendants
- heavily involved in social causes in recent years including fundraising for victims of 2010 Haiti earthquake
  and raising awareness of genocide in Darfur
- 2008 - appointed UN peace envoy

Vocabulary
Describing how you feel

1a Complete the grid with adjectives to describe how you would feel in each of the situations below.

1 You didn't get the job after an interview and don't feel very confident about your abilities.
2 You're in a really good mood and feeling optimistic.
3 You hate heights and you're at the top of a very tall building.
4 You've just received some bad news about a member of your family.
5 You've been unemployed for a long time and your partner has left you.
6 A large package arrives for you in the post one morning. You hadn't been expecting anything.
7 You read a funny story in the newspaper.
8 You woke up in a bad mood and the weather's awful.
9 You have to wake up very early after a late night.

b Complete the gaps using a word from exercise 1a.

1 I have had several late nights recently and I'm feeling very _____ .
2 Tom was very _____ last time I saw him because his girlfriend had just left him.
3 Sally has been _____ ever since she lost her job. What can we do to cheer her up? (depressed)
4 He can't swim, so going on the boat trip made him feel _____ .
5 My dad gets _____ when he is working and we make too much noise.
6 The joke really wasn't funny. Noone was _____ .
7 Even when things aren't going well, Julia is always _____ .
8 He's always been _____ . He needs to build up his self-confidence.
9 Young children are usually _____ and love finding out about new things.

Language focus 1
Forming adjectives

2a Complete the table.

noun	adjective	opposite adjective
hope	**1** *hopeful*	**2** *hopeless*
security	**3**	**4**
efficiency	**5**	**6**
success	**7**	**8**
solution	**9**	**10**
enthusiasm	**11**	**12**
comfort	**13**	**14**
patience	**15**	**16**
honesty	**17**	**18**

b 🎧 **2.1** Listen and check.

c Complete the gaps with adjectives from the table in exercise 2a.

1 After she got a new job, she was rather more *hopeful* about the future.
2 There was a(n) _____ silence when Luke's ex-girlfriend came into the room.
3 The train won't be here for another thirty minutes yet, so you'll just have to be _____ .
4 After her _____ third album, she decided to retire from her singing career.
5 I had really bad skin when I was a teenager, and this made me feel really _____ around girls.
6 To be completely _____ , I don't really like that dress. It makes you look old.
7 This is a fascinating book, it's about some of the biggest _____ crimes of the 20th century.
8 Sophie seemed very _____ . She had lots of interesting ideas as to how we could improve the department.

3 Find eight words with prefixes and two adjectives in the word square, using the clues to help you.

A	P	U	R	Y	A	V	E	E	S	G	R	T
E	U	R	O	S	N	P	O	P	E	P	P	D
P	N	O	N	S	T	O	P	R	M	R	O	I
T	D	I	S	T	I	O	U	E	P	O	S	S
L	E	N	D	R	C	R	E	F	A	D	T	S
M	R	T	S	E	L	K	O	L	T	E	G	A
B	C	R	R	S	O	I	L	I	O	M	R	T
F	O	V	E	S	C	R	I	G	R	O	A	I
H	O	R	V	E	K	W	Y	H	T	C	D	S
Z	K	R	E	D	W	A	H	T	Y	R	U	F
R	E	P	A	N	I	C	K	Y	E	A	A	I
S	D	R	I	O	S	U	N	S	A	C	T	E
T	S	E	L	F	E	M	P	L	O	Y	E	D
X	L	U	B	M	E	A	N	S	Y	S	A	O

1 We've been working _non-stop_ since eight this morning. Let's have a break.
2 I wish I wasn't so _____ on aeroplanes. Whenever there's turbulence, I start sweating and can't breathe.
3 You look _____ , can I give you a massage?
4 The quality of the food here has really gone downhill. We were really _____ with our meal.
5 Bill's _____ , so he doesn't have a boss and he can choose when he works.
6 To open a bottle, you always turn the top in an _____ direction.
7 Aung San Suu Kyi led the _____ movement in Myanmar (Burma).
8 The airport has a special _____ departure lounge for VIPs (Very Important Persons).
9 Emma's applying to do a _____ degree at Cambridge.
10 Waiter! I'm afraid this chicken is _____ .

4 Read the customer reviews for the 'Track your feelings' app and choose the correct alternatives.

TRACK YOUR FEELINGS

Customer reviews

TYF is a new app which helps you record how you feel at various points throughout the day. After a few days it provides a summary and suggestions which will help you become more self-aware and make better life choices.

⭐⭐⭐
A GOOD TIMEWASTER

This app is an ¹*amusing* / *amused* way to pass the time if you're ²*boring* / *bored*.

⭐
FORCES CLOSE

Keeps closing every time I try to load history – this is very ³*frustrating* / *frustrated*. Uninstalling.

⭐⭐⭐⭐⭐
AN EXCELLENT IDEA!

I was ⁴*fascinating* / *fascinated* to find out about myself. The possibilities are very ⁵*exciting* / *excited*.

⭐⭐
I WISH IT WASN'T SO HONEST!

This is an ⁶*interesting* / *interested* idea I think, but I was quite ⁷*disappointing* / *disappointed* to read what it said about me. It's all quite ⁸*depressing* / *depressed*!

Listen and read
Favourite films

A In *It's a Wonderful Life* with James Stewart, the scene that gets me is at the end when one guy says: 'To my big brother, George, the richest man in town.' It kills me, man. In the film, it's Christmas and James Stewart is in big trouble financially and he's going to be arrested and so he decides to kill himself. But then this angel comes down (only he looks like an ordinary guy) and shows him what life would have been like in his home town if he'd never lived. And he sees how his life has touched all these other lives and really made a difference. I watch most of the film with a lump in my throat. Brilliant!
Pete

C The opening of *Jaws*. It's all in the music, which is played on the cello. I expect everyone knows it. You start by seeing the sea from the point of view of a shark on the bottom of the sea bed. Then the scene moves to a beach and it's a sunny day and all these families are sunbathing and having a good time. Then there's a girl who goes into the water, and suddenly we're under the water again, looking at the girl's legs from the shark's point of view. Then suddenly she screams and she's dragged across the surface of the water before she disappears. I was on the edge of my seat. It's much more effective than showing the shark straightaway. And for the rest of the film, every time that music comes back you know something awful is going to happen.
Lisa

B One of the funniest moments, I think, is in the first Indiana Jones movie, *Raiders of the Lost Ark*, when Harrison Ford is trying to escape from his enemies. It takes place in an eastern market and Indiana is suddenly faced by an enormous man wearing a turban and carrying a huge sword. The man gives an awesome display of swordplay with this sword and you can see this feeling of panic passing over Indiana's face. Then he suddenly pulls out a gun and just shoots the guy. The first time I saw it, the audience broke out in a cheer. Amazing! Apparently, I read later, they were going to do a full fight, but Ford didn't want to spend hours in the scorching sun and it would have been very expensive, so he asked Spielberg (the director) if he could just shoot the guy and Spielberg agreed.
Mel

D *Star Wars*, every time. Not the later films, but the very first film right at the end when Luke Skywalker joins the rebel attack on the Death Star. The Death Star is this huge artificial 'moon' which is about to destroy the rebels' planet. And the only way to destroy it is for the X-wing pilots to fly down a narrow lane and hit a tiny opening. All of Luke's fellow-pilots are killed or their X-wings are damaged and it's up to him alone. He makes the decision to switch off his computer and use 'the Force' to find his target. 'Great shot, kid!' says Han Solo. 'That was one in a million!'
Steve

E The most I've ever cried in a movie was in *Pay it Forward*. It's about this kid, Trevor, and on his first day of school he gets this assignment: 'Think of an idea to change the world, and put it into practice.' And he has this idea that the world would change if everyone did good deeds for three other people, and then those three people would help three other people, and so on, and eventually it would spread right round the world. And then he gets killed trying to help a friend. And they ask everyone who has received an act of kindness or help as a result of his idea to light a candle and you see all these thousands of candles. I tell you, no one had a dry eye in the cinema.
Sandy

F *Jurassic Park*. The bit when the two kids are in the jeep and it's broken down and there's some water in the back and you hear this thumping noise, and all you see is the movement in the water and the fear in their eyes when they understand what it means. I saw it when I was about 11 and I was petrified. That was more frightening than actually seeing the Tyrannosaurus rex.
Anna

5a 🎧 **2.2** Listen to and/or read some people's opinions about films. Which question does each person answer?

In the movies
1 what makes you cry?
2 what makes you feel good?
3 what makes you scared?
A _1_ B ___ C ___ D ___ E ___ F ___

b Listen and/or read again and answer the questions.

Which films
1 are about someone's positive effect on other people? _____
2 involve a fight or battle? _____
3 depend a lot on the accompanying music or sound effects? _____

Vocabulary
Things that make you feel good

6 Match the statements in A with the ideas people are referring to in B.

A
1 'I go for a run three times a week, during my lunch hour at work.' _e_
2 'I hate the way that the government takes 20 per cent of my salary before I even get it.' ___
3 'I've just started my own business – it's great not having a boss!' ___
4 'I love my wife, she means everything to me.' ___
5 'It's good to know that I have a regular income and it's enough to live on.' ___
6 'It's so difficult to find a job in this area at the moment.' ___
7 'I've just done a course on computer programming and now I'm starting to make apps.' ___
8 'I wish I wasn't so shy sometimes, I'd like to find it easier to talk to other people.' ___
9 'I feel tired all the time.' ___
10 'I get bored very easily.' ___
11 'I think it's important to do your own thing, and not worry what other people say.' ___
12 'Having people who I know will be there for me, that's important.' ___

B
a I need to have variety and excitement in life.
b lack of sleep/exhaustion
c good friendships
d lack of confidence
e *I'm fit.*
f I'm unemployed.
g I'm an employer, not an employee.
h I hate paying taxes.
i I like being creative.
j financial security
k I have a strong relationship/marriage.
l I'm a non-conformist.

Language focus 2
Forming nouns and gerunds

7 Read the definitions from the *Longman Dictionary of Contemporary English* and write the correct nouns.

1 **m**_usician_ n [C] a person who plays a musical instrument for a job: *a talented young ...*
2 **t** ___ n [C] someone who is being trained for a job: *The new ... will start next week.*
3 **c** ___ n [C] the period of time when you are a child: *I had a happy ... .*
4 **e** ___ n [U] facts, objects or signs that make you believe that something exists or is true: *There is no ... of life on other planets.*
5 **g** ___ n [C] a person who plays a guitar
6 **b** ___ **o** ___ n [C] a small tool used for removing the metal lids from bottles
7 **a** ___ n [U] the cost of entrance to a concert, sports event, etc. : *... is free for children.*
8 **C** ___ n [U] a political system which has no different social classes and in which the government controls the production of all food and goods: *Do you believe in ... ?*
9 **c** ___ n [C] all the people who live in the same area, town, etc. : *an arts centre built to serve the whole ... .*
10 **e** ___ n [C] the pleasure that you get from something: *Acting has brought me enormous ... .*
11 **n** ___ n [U] being worried or frightened about something that may happen so that you cannot relax: *Minnelli's ... showed in her voice.*
12 **v** ___ n [C] Someone who eats only fruit, vegetables, eggs, etc. and does not eat meat or fish.

8a Complete the article with the positive or negative gerund form of the verbs in the box.

drink (x 2)   eat (x 2)   get   go (x̶ ̶2̶)
take (x 2)   talk

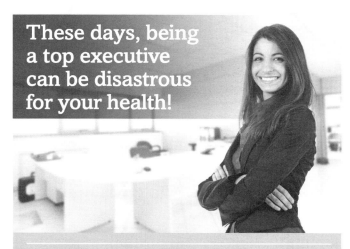

These days, being a top executive can be disastrous for your health!

We asked five managing directors how they coped. Their top ten tips for ways of keeping healthy and stress-free are:

1 _going_ to the gym three times a week.
2 _____ sensibly.
3 _____ alcohol at lunch.
4 _____ work home.
5 _____ at least seven hours' sleep each night.
6 _____ about business at home.
7 _____ mineral water instead of strong coffee.
8 _____ a daily 'power nap'.
9 _____ to bed after eleven o'clock during the week.
10 _____ fattening snacks between meals.

b Complete the second sentence so it has a similar meaning to the first. Use a gerund.

1 It can be expensive to eat out.
   _Eating out_____ can be expensive.
2 I find it easy to make new friends.
   _____ easy for me.
3 I hate it when people drop their rubbish in the street.
   I hate _____ .
4 It can be very stressful when you start a new job.
   _____ very stressful.
5 My mother-in-law can't stand people who smoke when she's eating.
   My mother-in-law _____ .
6 I find that a good way to relax is to have a nice long bath.
   _____ a good way to relax.

9 Read the extracts. Then complete the gaps using the correct form of the word given.

A

In a recent survey in Europe, [1]_employees_ were asked to list the things about 21st century living that cause [2]_____ .	EMPLOY ANXIOUS
Financial [3]_____ was the top answer, with over 60 per cent of people saying they feared becoming [4]_____ in the next year.	SECURE EMPLOY
In today's fast-paced workplace, many people said they suffer from lack of sleep and [5]_____ , which in turn causes erratic [6]_____ . Many people also answered that while they could accept [7]_____ from others, this sometimes caused a lack of [8]_____ in their own abilities.	EXHAUSTED BEHAVE CRITICISE CONFIDENT

B

[1]_Playing_ video games has for years been thought to have a negative effect on a child's [2]_____ . However, a recent [3]_____ into the effects of video on children has drawn a number of positives.	PLAY DEVELOP INVESTIGATE
[4]_____ have shown playing games in [5]_____ can help a child develop key skills such as [6]_____ , logic and problem – [7]_____ . Playing online games with other people can also help develop [8]_____ skills and the ability to make quick [9]_____ .	SCIENCE MODERATE MULTI-TASK SOLVE LEAD DECIDE
However, they were keen to stress that too much use of games can have a negative effect, causing an inability to distinguish between [10]_____ and fantasy, and eventual feelings of [11]_____ as they become more detached.	REAL LONELY

Pronunciation

Stressed and unstressed syllables in nouns

10 Complete the table with the words in the box.

aggression	~~anxiety~~	conformist	contentment
criticism	economist	loneliness	pessimism
reality	relationship	violence	

●●●●	●●●●	●●●	●●●
anxiety			

b 🎧 2.3 Listen and repeat the words, paying attention to the stress.

Writing

A description of something that happened to you

11a Chris has just moved to Bali with his girlfriend, Jodie to start a new job. Read his email to his friend Gary and choose the best summary below.

1 Chris wants to come home because he doesn't like his job.
2 Despite a few difficulties at first, Chris and Jodie are enjoying living there.
3 Chris loves living there but Jodie hates it.

b Complete the gaps in the email with adjectives.

c Choose one of the situations below and write an email to a friend, describing what happened and your feelings.

- something that happened to you which made you cry
- something you did which was really relaxing
- a time when you felt really happy
- something strange which happened to you
- a time when you tried something new

From: Chris

To: Gary

Subject: News from the frontier!

Hi mate!

Sorry it's taken me so long to get in touch, but things have been a bit crazy since I arrived here in Bali. The new job is great, and I'm really ¹op*timistic* about our future here. Jodie is just starting to settle in now – she was a bit ²pa_____ at first as we had trouble finding a place to live. We were both getting ³im_____ as we wanted to arrange somewhere quickly, and it was quite ⁴fr_____ having to do it in another language, but we've now found a lovely little place near the beach. The job is going well. My boss is really ⁵ch_____ and easy to get on with, and the other people I work with are really ⁶so_____ , too – we often go out after work together. I'm working really hard though and am ⁷ex_____ most days when I get home. Anyway, let me know when you're coming to visit!

All the best,

Chris

From:

To:

Subject:

Vocabulary
Mishaps

1a Read the descriptions of people's worst experiences and replace the words in bold with the correct form of a word/phrase in the box.

bang my head	break down	damage	drop
get confused	~~get lost~~	get on	get stuck
lock myself out	lose	miss	oversleep
run out of petrol	slip	spill	trip

The wedding

It was my friend Mike's wedding and it was in a church in the middle of nowhere about 40 km from Vancouver. Anyway, I didn't have a map and I [1]**became unable to find my way** and missed the ceremony. Then at the party afterwards I [2]**caught my foot on something** and [3]**dropped from my glass** my drink all over the bride's wedding dress! Worst of all, at the end of an uncomfortable evening, I realised I [4]**was unable to find** the piece of paper with the name of my hotel and so I had to sleep in my car.

Steve - Canada

1 *got lost*   **2** _____   **3** _____   **4** _____

The interview

I had an interview for a job I really wanted. Unfortunately, my alarm clock didn't go off and I [5]**slept too much**. I ran to the station but I was in such a rush that I [6]**became so I was not thinking clearly** and [7]**entered** the wrong train. I didn't arrive in Frankfurt until lunchtime and I was three hours late for the interview. Needless to say, I didn't get the job.

Helga - Germany

5 _____   **6** _____   **7** _____

The journey

I'd just been to a terrible party in Edinburgh and it was January. While I was there I [8]**accidentally let** my mobile **fall from my hand** on the floor and I [9]**nearly broke** it, so it didn't work. Well, on my way home, my car [10]**stopped working**, and my mobile wasn't working, so I had to walk. It had been snowing and the road was very icy. I [11]**slid with my feet** on the ice and [12]**knocked my head hard** on a tree. I woke up later in hospital with a very bad headache.

Pat - Scotland

8 _____   **9** _____   **10** _____
11 _____   **12** _____

The flight

It happened when I had to catch a plane from Madrid. I started off nice and early but then on the way there I [13]**used all my petrol and didn't have any left**. I managed to buy a can from a nearby garage, but when I got back to the car I saw my keys inside it and realized I had [14]**kept myself out by locking it**. A helpful mechanic from the garage found a key that opened the door and I continued on my journey. As I approached Madrid I [15]**became unable to move** in traffic for half an hour. As you can imagine, I [16]**failed to catch** my plane.

José - Spain

13 _____   **14** _____   **15** _____   **16** _____

b Complete the gaps with the correct form of a word or phrase from exercise 1a.

1 Hello, is that Park Street Garage? My car *has broken down*. Can you send someone to help?

2 Be careful or you _____ your coffee!

3 Eric _____ most of the meeting. He only arrived fifteen minutes before the end.

4 A: What happened?
   B: The floor was wet and I _____ and twisted my ankle. It's nothing serious.

5 You _____ the wrong train. This one is going to London. The Birmingham train is on platform nine.

6 The city centre is terrible. You can _____ in traffic jams for hours.

7 The hotel was so large that the first day Haifa worked there, she _____ and ended up in the laundry room.

8 Sorry to bother you but I _____ sugar. Can you lend me some?

9 I often _____ between Shaun and Ben. The twins look so similar.

10 I'm sorry I'm so late. My neighbours kept me awake last night and I _____ this morning.

11 Sheena felt so embarrassed when she _____ her glass and it smashed on the floor.

12 A: Are you OK?
    B: Yes, I just _____ my head on the cupboard door. I think I need to sit down for a moment.

13 It was dark in the living room and the police officer _____ over something and nearly fell.

14 She closed the door and then realised she _____ . Her key was still inside.

15 _____ anybody _____ a wallet? I found this in the hall.

16 If you _____ anything in the shop, you will have to pay for it.

Language focus 1
Narrative tenses

2 Use the prompts to write complete sentences. Choose the best past form of the verbs.

1

This / happen / one summer when three of us / travel / around Europe.

This happened one summer when three of us were travelling around Europe.

2

We / walk / around a town when a man / offer / to change our money.

_____
_____
_____
_____

3

A friend / warn / us never to change money on the street, but the man / look / honest, so we / decide / to take a chance.

_____
_____
_____
_____

4

He / pretend / to give me fifty notes but I / notice / that he / only give / me forty-eight, so I / ask / him to count them again.

_____
_____
_____
_____

5

Ten minutes later we / sit / in a café when I / realise / that he / trick / us.

_____
_____
_____
_____

6

When he / give / me back the money, he / replace / everything except the top two notes with newspaper!

_____
_____
_____
_____

3 Choose the best verb form in the sentences.

1 I couldn't believe that my brother **had sold** / had been selling his bike.

2 I discovered that Frank **had drunk** / **had been drinking** all the milk in the fridge.

3 The Minister of Transport, Carole Whitaker, told journalists that she **had resigned** / **had been resigning** from her job.

4 Carmen and Nando **had gone out** / **had been going out** for several years, so we were shocked when they split up.

5 The children were disappointed because Chris **hadn't come** / **hadn't been coming** to their party.

6 Kate was exhausted because she **'d worked** / **'d been working** so hard.

7 I felt extremely frustrated, as I **'d tried** / **'d been trying** to telephone his office for three days, with no success.

8 It was only when I got home that I realised to my horror that I **hadn't paid** / **hadn't been paying** for the meal.

4 Read these letters about life's biggest disappointments from a teen magazine. Complete the gaps with the correct form of the verbs in the boxes.

My sister ¹<u>cancelled</u> her wedding three days before it was due to happen. I ²_____ to make her change her mind because I ³_____ to wearing the dress that my mum ⁴_____ for me for weeks. On the day she was supposed to get married, I ⁵_____ into her room while she ⁶_____ a bath and ⁷_____ her favourite dress into little pieces.

Liz, aged twelve

~~cancel~~	cut	go	have	look forward
make	try		

My dad is always playing practical jokes on us, and the worst one ever was the lottery one. We ⁸_____ the lottery for years and we ⁹_____ anything, so when my dad ¹⁰_____ us a lottery ticket with the winning numbers from that night on it, we ¹¹_____ believe our luck! Later, when we ¹²_____ what to spend the money on, he ¹³_____ us the ticket was a fake he ¹⁴_____ . My mum ¹⁵_____ to him for weeks!

Joseph, aged eleven

---

can't	do	make	not speak
not win	plan	show	tell

Vocabulary
Crime and punishment

5 Complete the newspaper stories with the crimes.

A

NO 'ENCORE' FOR POP STAR

Singer Chris T. was arrested for ¹<u>drink-driving</u> last night. He was on his way home from a nightclub when his car hit a tree. He and his passenger had no injuries, but he failed a breath test when police arrived on the scene. He was also later charged with ²p_____ of i_____ d_____ when he was searched on arriving at the police station.

B

BRITAIN'S WORST TEENAGER?

A 13-year-old girl from Birmingham has been called 'Britain's worst teenager' this year. She has ³p_____ t_____ over 200 times this school year, and also been accused of ⁴a_____ – s_____ b_____ by local residents in the street where she lives, including writing ⁵g_____ on their houses.

C

FURY AS LOCAL PERFORMER ARRESTED

There has been outrage after a local woman was arrested for ⁶b_____ while playing her guitar and singing to commuters at the local railway station. The 28-year-old woman was popular with morning travellers, with one passenger saying she 'brightened up my mornings'.

6 Match the correct form of the words/phrases in the box with the descriptions of what punishments the people in exercise 5 received. Match the punishments with the people.

---

get a suspended sentence	give community service
~~let off with a warning~~	lose his/her licence
taken into care	

---

1 This person wasn't punished, but told not to perform in public again, or she would receive a punishment next time.
   Punishment: <u>She was let off with a warning.</u>   <u>C</u>

2 This person was removed from her family and put into a special home. She was ordered to spend 25 hours cleaning the streets.
   Punishments: She was _____ and _____ .   ___

3 This person had the document which allows them to drive taken away and was told that if they commit any more crimes in the next year, they would go to prison.
   Punishments: He _____ and _____ .   ___

Language focus 2
Continuous aspect in other tenses

7 Complete the extract with the Present perfect simple or continuous form of the verbs in brackets.

Shridhar Chillal, who lives near Bombay, [1]*has been* (be) in the Guinness Book of Records for the last twenty years for having the world's longest nails – one is more than a hundred centimetres long. He [2]_____ (grow) them for more than fifty years and has to be extremely careful in case he damages them. However, recently he [3]_____ (feel) very tired: 'My nails are very heavy and I [4]_____ (not had) a full night's sleep for the last few years, worrying about damaging them. I [5]_____ (never hold) my new grandson for fear of breaking them, and now the nerves in my left hand [6]_____ (die) because I [7]_____ (never use) it. I [8]_____ (think) about it a lot recently and now I [9]_____ (decide) to cut off my nails and sell them to a museum.'

8 Complete the email with the Future simple or continuous form of the verbs in the box.

be	bring	have	look after	not forget
not work	~~pack~~	phone	send	wander

Hi Julian,

Just a quick email before we go away. We're off to Morocco tomorrow. I can't wait, but I'm nowhere near ready yet. I think I [1] *'ll be packing* all night! I'm sure by the time I get on the plane I [2] _____ exhausted!

Still, just think, this time next week I [3] _____ round the old city or maybe I [4] _____ a swim in the hotel pool. The great thing is I [5] _____ I promise I [6] _____ you a postcard and I [7] _____ you something back from Marrakech.

As I said, Sandra [8] _____ Tigger from Monday to Friday but if you could feed him on Saturday and Sunday, that would be brilliant. You [9] _____ to give him some milk as well, will you?

Thanks again and I [10] _____ you as soon as we get back.

Trish xx

9 Choose the correct alternative to complete the sentences below.

1 Where are you? I*'ll ring* /(*'ve been ringing*)/ *'ve rang* you for the last hour!
2 They*'ve been staying* / *'ll stay* / *stay* with friends while the repairs are carried out. That's why they aren't here.
3 I think I*'ll go out* / *'ve been going out* / *'ll be going out* for dinner with my boyfriend tonight.
4 You look exhausted! What **will you do** / **will you be doing** / **have you been doing**?
5 Don't call me between 10 and 11 tomorrow, I*'ll give* / *'ll be giving* / **have given** a presentation.
6 That's the second time I*'ll say* / *'ve been saying* / *'ve said* 'hello' and she's ignored me. So rude!
7 Have you heard? Ella*'s won* / *'ll be winning* / *'s been winning* an award for the project she did last year.
8 Think of me this time tomorrow – I*'ll take* / *'ll be taking* / *'ve taken* my driving test.

Vocabulary
Headlines

10 Match a beginning from A with an ending from B. Replace the words in bold in the headlines below with the correct word in the box.

back	calls	death toll	set to
~~severe~~	vows		

A

1 Storm causes ~~very serious~~ damage   *severe*   c
2 Energy company **probably going to** announce ___
3 Top celebrities **support** change to ___
4 **Number of people dead** in earthquake ___
5 New **demands** for tighter gun ___
6 President **promises** to build ___

B

a rises to 70.
b more schools.
c to local homes.
d controls after shooting.
e privacy laws.
f 2,000 new jobs

Listen and read
Winners and losers

11a 🎧 **3.1** Listen to and/or read about three unlucky experiences and answer the question.

Who lost the most money? _____

b Listen to and/or read the texts again. Are these statements true (T) or false (F)?

1 Mrs Song gave the teddy bear to the sale by mistake. _____
2 There were plenty of objects for sale at the jumble sale. _____
3 The syndicate members didn't take the robbery seriously at first. _____
4 The party was only for the syndicate members. _____
5 Eric Culbertson was going to propose in a hotel. _____
6 The couple are now engaged. _____

c Who made the following statements?

1 'They seemed very pleased with it.'
   The person who sold the teddy at the jumble sale.
2 'Yes, I will.' _____
3 'It's devastating but we shall just have to try again.' _____
4 'She should have told me.' _____
5 'It's just sad to work that hard, to plan all that, then to have it all ruined.' _____
6 'They were rather foolish to let everyone know what was going to happen.' _____
7 'I told nobody at first, then decided that the buyer is more likely to return the money if they know who it belongs to.' _____
8 'Nobody move!' _____

Family accidentally sold teddy bear containing $50,000 in cash

An Alaskan family accidentally sold an old teddy bear containing $50,000 in cash at a church jumble sale. Wan Song had borrowed the money for her husband's cancer treatment and had hidden it inside the bear. But she hadn't told her husband, Inhong Song, who gave the bear to the church sale in their home town of Anchorage.

Mrs Song is now appealing for whoever bought the bear to return it to the family. She had borrowed the money from friends and relatives without her husband's knowledge, to pay for surgery he needed for cancer of the pancreas.

For safekeeping, she wrapped the money in foil and sewed it inside one of their children's old teddy bears which she then hid at the back of a cupboard. Meanwhile, the family decided to help their local church jumble sale and Mrs Song packed up some items, which her husband delivered.

But when the jumble sale began to run out of items, he went back to the house, found the bear and brought it to the sale.

An older woman with two girls reportedly bought it for a dollar.

Lottery syndicate robbed of winnings at celebration party

An Italian lottery syndicate won and then lost a fortune when members were robbed at gunpoint as they divided up their $60,000 winnings. Five masked gunmen burst into the celebration party at a social club as the money was being handed out in envelopes, and grabbed the cash before escaping in a waiting car.

Syndicate organiser Vincenzo Paviglianiti said: 'We were just about to start handing out the money when five men burst in wearing masks. At first everyone laughed because they thought it was part of the party, but then the men started shouting and telling everyone to get on the floor and not to move. It was only after one of them fired a shot into the air that everyone realised it wasn't a joke. They took all the money, but at least no one was hurt.'

Police said the forty-strong syndicate may have been the victim of its own generosity after advertising the party on posters at Reggio Calabria in southern Italy. A spokesman said: 'The syndicate had put up posters and balloons in the streets around their local social club and had invited neighbours to come and celebrate their win with them. In effect, the robbers knew what was going to happen and that the money was going to be divided up at the celebration.'

Man loses $10,000 engagement ring in taxi

A man who'd saved up for over a year to buy a $10,000 engagement ring for his girlfriend lost it in a taxi in Chicago. Eric Culbertson put the ring – a platinum band with a round-cut diamond – into his wallet as he got into the taxi. He was taking girlfriend Krista Saputo to a restaurant where he'd intended to propose. But after leaving the taxi, he realised the ring was no longer in his wallet.

The twenty-eight-year-old had paid for a suite at a city hotel and arranged for chocolate-covered strawberries and champagne for their arrival. He'd also booked a table at a restaurant in the city, says the *Chicago Tribune*.

The following day, the couple travelled to Pleasant Prairie, Wisconsin for a family reunion. There, Culbertson bought a twenty-five-dollar cubic zirconia ring and asked Saputo to marry him. She accepted.

Language live
Dealing with unexpected problems

12a Complete the conversations with the missing words.

1 A: I'm sorry sir, but there's no reservation under that name.
   B: [1]*What do you mean*? My company made the reservation last week over the phone.
   A: Well, I'm sorry, but we have no record of that.
   B: Well, [2]i_____ n_____ my f_____ that you haven't recorded it properly. Do you have no available rooms?
   A: Well, let me see what I can do.

2 A: What's this? A parking ticket?
   B: Yes, sir. You've overstayed the 45 minutes that you paid for.
   A: [3]I u_____ t_____ , but I'm only two minutes late!
   B: Sorry sir, but you cannot park for longer than the time you pay for.
   A: [4]Can I m_____ a s_____ ? Why d_____ I pay for another 45 minutes now, and then everyone's happy.
   B: OK, just this once, then.

3 A: That'll be £175, please.
   B: What? But you haven't repaired the washing machine. [5]I don't t_____ that's f_____ .
   A: I realise that, but we charge £175 for a call-out at the weekend.
   B: But [6]t_____ is r_____ ! I work during the week, and I'm only here at the weekend!
   A: Look, I'll tell you what. Let me repair it, then we can discount this charge from the repair bill.

b 🎧 **3.2 Listen and check.**

Pronunciation
Identifying the speaker's feelings

13 🎧 **3.3 Listen to the expressions from exercise 12 said twice. In which one does the speaker sound annoyed and in which does he/she sound calm? Write *a* or *b* below.**

1 What do you mean?
   annoyed *a*   calm *b*
2 Well, it's not my fault ...
   annoyed ___   calm ___
3 I understand that, ...
   annoyed ___   calm ___
4 Can I make a suggestion?
   annoyed ___   calm ___
5 I don't think that's fair.
   annoyed ___   calm ___
6 But this is ridiculous.
   annoyed ___   calm ___

Writing
A narrative

14a Read Marisol's story quickly. Which sentence (A, B or C) is true?

A She went on holiday to Norway and hired a car. ___
B They went on a day trip and she nearly missed her flight home. ___
C They went on a day trip and crashed because of bad weather. ___

The Most Frightening Day of My Life

Several years ago
I was spending Christmas in Tenerife, in the Canary Islands. My brother José was working there and he couldn't get any time off to come home, so I spent the holiday with him. We decided to go up Mount Teide, a volcano in the centre of the island, and officially the second largest mountain in Europe. This was the last day of my visit, so we hired a little car for the day – I couldn't drive, but my brother could.

José and I set off in brilliant sunshine, but it got much colder and by the time we reached the crater of Mount Teide it was snowing. All the restaurants, hotels and petrol stations at the top of the volcano were shut, and we had almost run out of petrol. I started getting really worried because I had to catch the plane home that evening, and if I didn't, I would have to pay for a new ticket. So José decided to do something incredibly dangerous – he switched off the engine of the car and freewheeled down the other side of the mountain.

He did this for several kilometres, round hairpin bends on dangerous, icy roads. I was absolutely petrified, but for some reason I didn't tell him to stop.

My worst nightmare happened: the car slipped on the road and the two front wheels went over the edge. We were very lucky that the rest of the car didn't go over. We sat in the car, not daring to move and freezing cold, waiting for someone to come past. A car came round the corner and out jumped three enormous men. Without saying a word, the three men surrounded the car and literally lifted it back on the road. My brother and I got out to thank them, but the three men just repeated 'Norway' several times – we assumed that that was where they came from – then got back into their car and drove off. We were so relieved we could have kissed them! We got back into our car and continued down the side of the mountain. I have never felt so happy in my life as when we reached the town at the bottom. We went straight to a petrol station and filled up. The petrol station was owned by a Norwegian company!

b Improve the story by inserting these adverbial phrases in the best place. They are in the correct order.

~~Several years ago~~   unfortunately   One day
very quickly   For some reason   At this point,
All of a sudden   for ages,   Eventually,
By this stage   Ironically,

c Write a story about a journey that you've been on. Describe where you went, what happened and how you felt. Use adverbial phrases from exercise 14b.

Vocabulary
Mental skills

1 Match one of the mental skills from the box to each situation below.

creativity and imagination   emotional intelligence
~~mathematical skills~~   memory   musical ability
organisational skills   problem-solving skills
visual/spatial intelligence

1 You are comparing prices per kilo of different vegetables when shopping.
mathematical skills

2 You are lost in a city and using a map to work out where you are.
_____

3 You have started a new job and are trying to remember everyone's names.
_____

4 You take part in a karaoke contest.
_____

5 Your daughter tells you she knows a secret about someone that might get them in trouble, and she doesn't know what to do.
_____

6 You are arranging your wedding.
_____

7 You are deciding how to redecorate a room in your house.
_____

8 You usually drive to work but your car has broken down and you might be late for work.
_____

Language focus 1
Use and non-use of the passive

2 Read the clues and find the answer.

1 It's grown.
It's drunk hot or cold.
It's sometimes sweetened,
but it's never roasted.
What is it?
_tea_____

2 It was built by a king to show his love for his dead wife.
It's visited by thousands of people every year.
It's made of white stone.
It's been called the most beautiful building in the world.
What is it?
_____

3 It's watched but never read.
It's switched on and off.
It's been blamed for the death of conversation.
It was invented by John Logie Baird.
What is it?
_____

4 It was invented in England.
It's played all over the world.
Songs are sung about different teams.
Many competitions have been won by Brazil.
What is it?
_____

5 He is known all over the world.
He was elected in 2008 and again in 2012.
He was born in Hawaii.
Many campaigns on healthy eating have been introduced by his wife.
Who is he?
_____

6 It's governed by a mayor.
It was founded by the Romans.
The Olympics were held there in 2012.
It's visited by millions of tourists every year.
Where is it?
_____

3a Complete the sentences with the correct passive form of the verb in brackets, and underline the correct answer.

1 Several famous pictures of water lilies _were painted_ (paint) by _____ .
  a Renoir   **b** Monet
2 Portuguese _____ (speak) in _____ .
  a Chile   **b** Brazil
3 The structure of DNA _____ (know) about for more than _____ .
  a ninety years   **b** sixty years
4 At the moment, more _____ .
  a tablets   **b** calculators
  _____ (buy) than ever before.
5 New Zealand _____ originally _____ (inhabit) by _____ .
  a Aborigines   **b** Maoris
6 The 2022 World Cup _____ (not hold) in _____ .
  a Brazil   **b** Qatar
7 Humans _____ already _____ (arrive) in the Americas before Christopher Columbus 'discovered' them in _____ .
  a 1592   **b** 1492
8 The part of James Bond in the 2012 film, *Skyfall* _____ (play) by _____ .
  a Ralph Fiennes   **b** Daniel Craig

b 🎧 **4.1** Listen and check.

4 Complete the extracts with the correct active or passive form of the verbs in brackets.

A

Adfen Plus [1]_is recommended_ (recommend) for those times when you [2]_____ (need) powerful relief from pain. The tablets [3]_____ (specially / formulate) to make them easy to swallow. Each tablet [4]_____ (contain) ibuprofen BP 200 mg and aspirin. As with other pain relievers, Adfen Plus should [5]_____ (not / take) if you have any stomach disorders.

B

This little-known castle [1]_____ (only recently / open) its doors to the public, and Qualtours [2]_____ (offer) special reductions for this month only. The tour [3]_____ (include) the living quarters, the library, the kitchens and the gardens. The size of each tour [4]_____ (limit) to 12 people. Bookings may [5]_____ (make) in advance by telephone.

C

Licorice [1]_____ (use) by mankind for thousands of years. In China in 3000 BC, licorice [2]_____ (believe) to have amazing powers and [3]_____ (use) in certain religious ceremonies. People [4]_____ (believe) that it could [5]_____ (protect) the dead from evil spirits.

D

An outbreak of food poisoning at a top London hotel [1]_____ (investigate) last night. More than 15 guests at a business lunch at the Stanmore Hotel [2]_____ (complain) of nausea during the afternoon, after eating shellfish which doctors later found [3]_____ (not / properly / clean). Ten people [4]_____ (currently / treat) in hospital, but most of them expect [5]_____ (send) home later today.

5 Tick (✓) the best way of continuing after each sentence, depending on what the main focus is.

1 Niamh O'Connor has won the Best Actress award at the National Film Awards this year.
  a Sean Curtis gave the award to her.
  b She was given the award by Sean Curtis. ✓
2 My brother-in-law is very rich.
  a A house in Barbados has just been bought by him.
  b He's just bought a house in Barbados.
3 What are we going to do about Lexi?
  a We should discuss her behaviour with her.
  b Her behaviour should be discussed with her.
4 What's this song? I really like it!
  a It's by The Redtones.
  b The Redtones wrote it.
5 Should I leave a tip?
  a No, service is included.
  b No, they include service.
6 Alan Cook has been appointed CEO of Niceton Bank.
  a A salary of over $1 million will be paid to him.
  b He will be paid a salary of over $1 million.
7 Why isn't Clarke playing?
  a The referee sent him off for a bad tackle.
  b He was sent off for a bad tackle.
8 The gang appeared in court today.
  a They'd been arrested last night.
  b They'd been arrested last night by the police.

Listen and read
Driving each other crazy

6a Write down two adjectives to describe male drivers and two adjectives to describe female drivers.

_____ _____ _____ _____

b 🎧 **4.2** Listen to and/or read the article. Put a tick (✓) next to the things you agree with.

Driving Each Other Crazy

There's a well-known joke: A woman is driving down a motorway and her husband phones her on her mobile. 'Darling, be careful!' he screams, 'I've just heard there's a car driving the wrong way on the motorway near where you are.' 'It's not just one car,' she says, 'there are hundreds of them!'

And here's another one: a man is driving his daughter and they are stuck in traffic. The little girl says, 'I have a question.' 'What is it?' asks her father. 'When you're driving, are YOU ever the stupid idiot?'

Why do we laugh at these jokes? Is it because we recognise some truth in them? A lot of people seem to think that men and women do display quite different characteristics when it comes to driving, and in general, both male and female drivers tend to be quite critical of the opposite sex.

'Men are too confident in their own abilities. They never listen, they never need a map. They're always sure they know the way,' says Cathy, whose husband rarely lets her drive the car. 'They tend to drive too close to the car in front and they're incredibly impatient. If there's a car in front, they have to pass it even if it doesn't make a difference to their overall speed. I think it's some sort of territorial thing – you know, they have to be king of the road and everybody else on the road is an idiot.'

Danielle, a businesswoman who drives a BMW, agrees: 'Men never indicate before they turn left and they tend to brake at the very last minute. If I'm in a car with a man, I often feel quite nervous. I'd much rather be driven by a woman.'

It seems as if insurance companies would agree. Apparently, whilst the number of accidents men and women have tend to be about equal, the accidents which involve women are generally relatively minor and they are therefore less expensive to insure. In contrast, men tend to have more serious accidents and the worst offenders are young men, aged between 18 and 25.

What do men think about women? Interestingly, one of their main concerns is about women as passengers: 'Women passengers can't keep quiet,' says Paul, a retired architect. 'You know: "You're going too fast", "Can you see that pedestrian?", "Didn't you see that traffic light?" or "I feel sick. Can't you go straight?" There's always some comment.'

Pete agrees: 'And women are hopeless with directions. I think it's because they're nervous about going to new places. I reckon men are better at finding new places and women are better at finding places they've been to before.'

Certainly it seems to be the case that if a man fails to follow directions, it's because his female passenger did not convey them properly. But what about women's driving? Pete again: 'My girlfriend has some strange habits, like switching on the windscreen wipers as a signal that she intends to turn right. Then she gets annoyed when she's driving and I 'brake' – you know, put my foot down as if I'm braking – when she's going round corners. I mean, one of us has to!'

Despite men's generally high opinion of their own driving skills, a report published in 2004 came down firmly in favour of women drivers. According to the report, women score more highly than men on almost all counts. These included driving within the speed limits, overtaking safely and conducting different manoeuvres successfully, including signalling in good time, reversing and braking quickly. They also had a better awareness of other drivers on the road. There was only one aspect of driving where women did not perform as successfully as men and that was – no surprise here – the ability to park their cars.

When it comes to driving, it seems that men and women may indeed come from different planets!

c According to the article, are these statements true (T) or false (F)?

1 The woman was driving the wrong way down the motorway. *T*
2 The father thought he was better than other drivers. ____
3 Cathy does nearly all the driving in her family. ____
4 Cathy thinks men overtake other cars in order to reach their destination quicker. ____
5 Danielle thinks men are not very considerate of other drivers. ____
6 Older men are probably more popular with insurance companies than young men. ____
7 Paul seems to be a very careful driver. ____
8 Pete thinks men are better than women at following directions to somewhere new. ____
9 Many men think it's not their fault if they get directions wrong. ____
10 Pete's girlfriend sometimes uses the wrong lever when she's signalling. ____
11 She also brakes too much when going round a corner. ____
12 Men are better at parking than women. ____

Wordspot
mind

7 Insert a missing word from the box into each
sentence below.

absent	~~don't~~	helping	her	never	on
open	own	speaks	the	up	went

don't
  y
1 I mind doing the cooking if you do the washing-up.
2 She's very tolerant. She's quite minded about
   things.
3 I'm sorry. I'm not very good company this
   evening. I've got something my mind.
4 Has Mrs Chen changed mind? I thought she was
   staying at the Hilton.
5 Although I'd met Vladimir several times before,
   my mind blank and I couldn't remember his name.
6 You've lost my pen? Oh, mind. It wasn't valuable.
7 Would you mind me with my suitcases?
8 Dave is so minded. He got all the way to the
   theatre and then realised he'd got the wrong date.
9 I made my mind not to take the job.
10 Mind gap between the train and the platform.
11 Yes, I got a pay rise, but no, I'm not going to tell
   you how much. Mind your business!
12 My new secretary is surprisingly honest. She
   certainly her mind.

Language focus 2
Passive forms with *have* and *get*

8 Put the words in order to make questions.

1 your / often / do / have / How / serviced / you / car ?
   How often do you have your car serviced?
2 hair / you / dyed / Have / ever / your / had ?
   _____
3 last / When / your / tested / did / get / eyes / you ?
   _____
4 you / famous / photo / ever / Have / someone /
   with / your / had / taken ?
   _____
5 to / hair / differently / like / have / you / your / cut /
   Would ?
   _____
6 house / broken / your / Has / into / ever / been ?
   _____

9a Complete the conversations using the correct form
of *have* or *get* with the verbs in the box.

check	clean	~~cut~~	print	publish	put up

1 A: You look different. Have you *had* your hair *cut* ?
   B: Yes. What do you think?
2 A: You look pleased with yourself.
   B: Yes, I've finally _____ an article _____ in the
      local newspaper!
3 A: Can you _____ these business cards _____ for
      me?
4 A: Oh no! I'm so sorry – all over your shirt!
   B: It really doesn't matter.
   A: No, I'll pay for you to _____ it _____ .
   B: Yes, when do you want them done by?
5 A: I'm sorry about the noise.
   B: Yes, what's going on?
   A: We _____ some shelves _____ .
6 A: I'm not sure about this contract they want me to
      sign.
   B: Me neither. I'd _____ it _____ by a lawyer, if I
      were you.

b 🎧4.3 Listen and check.

Vocabulary
Personal characteristics

10 Megan is Personnel Officer in a busy hospital. She has just interviewed five people for the position of Senior Nurse. Read her notes and write two adjectives from the box next to each candidate.

arrogant   attention-seeking   calm   extrovert
good in a team   hot-tempered   ~~humorous~~
introvert   needy   rebellious

SARAH: I liked her because she seemed very friendly and positive; she smiled a lot during the interview and even made a few jokes. I got the impression that she didn't like being told what to do, as she kept telling me about how she couldn't agree with her previous boss.

humorous _____

JUAN: At first I thought what a nice man – seemed very confident and outgoing, but then when I asked him why he'd left his last job and if he had had any problems, he got quite angry. We can't have someone who can't control their emotions.

_____   _____

MARIA: Very popular with previous colleagues and easy to get on with. When I posed some hypothetical problems to her, she dealt with them efficiently, without panicking.

_____   _____

LAURA: No. She seemed to think we should be begging her to join us . . . a big ego! She seemed to feel that she didn't always get credit for what she said were her ideas, too.

_____   _____

JIM: Seemed very shy and uncomfortable around other people. I think he'd be a problem because he kept asking a lot of questions, about very basic things. I think he'd need a lot of support.

_____   _____

11 Find eight personal characteristics in the word square, using the clues to help you.

P	S	F	T	K	S	S	R	I	E	J	T	V	E	E
C	O	M	U	T	H	S	S	N	I	U	O	W	X	E
Q	U	E	R	K	U	M	U	D	A	T	I	O	P	R
U	N	C	O	M	M	U	N	I	C	A	T	I	V	E
W	E	E	Y	P	O	R	V	V	M	E	I	O	D	S
J	E	A	L	O	U	S	E	I	Y	Z	J	E	R	I
H	O	D	T	F	R	Y	J	D	S	T	R	E	I	L
A	E	D	D	U	L	P	L	U	D	E	R	S	W	I
A	R	G	U	M	E	N	T	A	T	I	V	E	E	E
E	D	J	D	R	S	C	G	L	Y	K	G	S	S	N
P	O	T	E	R	S	W	U	I	A	U	A	A	B	T
I	N	R	T	R	E	P	A	S	D	E	W	O	N	E
S	E	L	T	A	L	K	A	T	I	V	E	I	V	E
S	E	L	F	S	U	F	F	I	C	I	E	N	T	G
E	J	L	Y	M	D	T	H	C	U	E	G	H	D	R

1 Unhappy because someone else has something which you want. *jealous*
2 Difficult to talk to, finds it difficult to express ideas. _____
3 Likes arguing, often tries to be controversial. _____
4 Talks a lot. _____
5 Independent, doesn't rely on other people. _____
6 Serious, doesn't find things funny. _____
7 Does things in his/her own way, has different opinions from other people. _____
8 Strong, able to recover easily from a difficult situation or problem. _____

Pronunciation
Stress patterns

12a Complete the table with the words in the box.

~~ability~~   absent-minded   argumentative
creativity   extrovert   humorous   logic
needy   open-minded   rebellious   resilient
self-sufficient   spatial   talkative   uncommunicative

●●●●	●●●●●●	●●●●●●
ability		

●●	●●●	●●●●

b ⏺ 4.4 Listen and repeat the words, paying attention to the stress.

Writing
An email home

13a Lauren is travelling in Indonesia. Read her email and choose the correct alternatives.

○ ○ ○

From: Lauren

To: Mum and Dad

Subject: First email home!

¹**Hi!**/ *Good afternoon*.

How is everyone at home? It all seems a million miles away now. I've been in Indonesia for the last three weeks. Sorry I haven't written yet but it's been really ²*quiet / **hectic** here, there's always so much to see.

Java is amazing, we landed in Jakarta last week and have been working our way slowly across to Bali. Travelling here is quite an experience, it's very cheap but public transport can be quite complicated – planning how to get somewhere is often a test of ³*logic / emotional intelligence*!

The people I'm travelling with are really friendly, but we don't always agree on what to do. Lucy is sometimes quite ⁴*needy / self-sufficient* to be honest, and tends to follow us around everywhere we go, whereas Jodie can be a bit ⁵*humorous / humourless* at times and takes things very seriously. I ⁶*don't really mind / have something on my mind,* though. Despite our differences, it's good to be travelling with other people and I appreciate the company.

The best thing about this trip is that life here is so different and every day is a new experience. I'm really glad I ⁷*spoke my mind / made up my mind* to come here.

Anyway, ⁸*give my Grandma to love / give my love to Grandma* and I'll write again soon.

Lauren xxx

b Imagine you have been travelling for three weeks. Write your first email home. Think about:

- Where you are
- What the other people are like
- The best/worst thing about the place you are in now
- How you are feeling about the trip

● ○ ○ New Message

From:

To:

Subject:

05 FACE TO FACE

Vocabulary
Getting together

1a Use the clues to complete the grid.

(crossword grid with letters S, C, H, O, O, L, R, E, U, N, I, O, N spelling SCHOOL REUNION vertically)

1 I went to a _school reunion_ last night, and it was great to see so many of my ex-classmates. (2 words)

2 Some of the _____ had come all the way from Hong Kong just for the wedding.

3 I have an important business meeting with some _____ this afternoon.

4 In 2012, we had a big street party with all our _____ .

5 Could you make an _____ for me to see Mr Ikegame some time tomorrow?

6 I'm trying to organise a little _____ at my place on Saturday – can you come? (2 words)

7 All our friends and _____ are going to be at the wedding.

8 When Kristin passed her exams, we went out for a _____ at her favourite restaurant. (2 words)

9 Each member of the United Nations may send five _____ to the General Assembly.

10 Aaron moved into his new apartment months ago and he still hasn't had a _____ party. (2 words)

11 Uma and Carl have arranged a _____ for me with a friend of theirs – I'm really nervous. (2 words)

12 There have been angry demonstrations outside the building where the two presidents are having their _____ meeting.

13 Representatives from over a hundred countries attended the International Peace _____ .

14 I'm involved in a really lively discussion on an _____ at the moment about the latest series of _Game of Thrones_. (2 words)

b Write four sentences using words from exercise 1a so they are true for you.

1 _____
2 _____
3 _____
4 _____

Language focus 1
Review of future forms

2 Complete the conversations with _'ll_ or _going to_ using the verbs in brackets.

1 A: Can I speak to Miss Beatty in accounts?
B: Yes, I _'ll put_ (put) you through.

2 A: My calculator's not working and I need it for the exam.
B: Don't panic, I _____ (lend) you mine.

3 A: You look very tired – you need a break.
B: Yes, I _____ (have) two days off next week. Mr Brumfit agreed to it.

4 A: We've got a bit of a problem, there's a strong smell of gas in the house.
B: Right, madam, I _____ (send) someone round immediately.

5 A: So what's the kitchen like?
B: It's nice and big but it's a bit dark, so we _____ (paint) it yellow.

6 A: Your exam results weren't very good, were they?
B: I know, but I've decided I _____ (work) much harder next year.

7 A: Do you want to have a party for your twenty-first birthday?
B: Oh I don't know. I _____ (think) about it.

8 A: Have you decided what to do about the house?
B: Yes. We _____ (not sell) it after all.

9 A: Did you get an email from the accounts department this morning?
B: I don't know, I _____ (check) my inbox.

10 A: Are you and Jason friends again yet?
B: No, I _____ (never speak) to him again!

3 In many situations we can use either the Present continuous or *going to*. In these sentences, cross out the Present continuous where it is not possible.

1 Paula *is going to become* / *is becoming* a specialist in heart surgery when she finishes her training.
2 I'm *going to have* / *having* a party on Saturday. Would you like to come?
3 I'm *really going to enjoy* / *really enjoying* the concert tomorrow night.
4 My husband's *going to see* / *seeing* the doctor on Friday.
5 What time is your sister's plane *going to leave* / *leaving*?
6 Who are you *going to meet* / *meeting* for lunch today?
7 One day I'm *going to meet* / *meeting* the girl of my dreams.
8 Peter keeps telling us he's *going to make* / *making* a million pounds before he's forty.
9 We're *going to spend* / *spending* the holidays with some friends from Canada.
10 When are you *going to learn* / *learning* some table manners?

4 In four of the sentences below, the Present simple is not used correctly to talk about the future. Find the mistakes and correct them.

1 What time does your train get in? ✓
   _____
2 Everything on the menu sounds delicious, but I have the chicken risotto.
   _____
3 You break that window if you're not careful.
   _____
4 What are you going to do when you retire?
   _____
5 Wait a minute – I help you with those bags.
   _____
6 As soon as I get home, I promise I phone you.
   _____
7 I'll get some more steaks in case Jan and Ian stay for dinner.
   _____

5a Sharon is worried about a barbecue she is organising, and her friend Rhona is reassuring her. Put *S* next to Sharon's comments and *R* next to Rhona's.

1 I don't know why I decided to have a barbecue this afternoon, I _bet_ it'll rain. _S_
2 I'm never _____ get these salads ready in time. ___
3 Slow down a bit! You're _____ cut yourself with that knife if you're not careful. ___
4 Stop worrying about the food. _____ it'll all taste wonderful. ___
5 These steaks _____ take a while to cook – they're really thick. Are you going to put them on the barbecue first? ___
6 _____ that half the people I've invited won't come. ___
7 Well, at least fifteen people have told me they're coming. And _____ some of your neighbours will turn up, too. ___
8 Marc said he'd bring me some extra chairs but he'll _____ forget. ___
9 People _____ to want plenty of soft drinks. Shall I get some more juice from the shop? ___
10 There's just so much to do. I'm _____ forget something. ___

b Complete the sentences in 5a with a word or phrase in the box.

almost certainly   are likely   ~~bet~~   certain to
going to (x2)   I'm sure (x2)   may well
there's a good chance that

Listen and read
The weird ways people meet

6a 🎧 5.1 Listen to and/or read the article. Who …

1 thought he might not have been thinking properly when they met? _Nick McKiddie_

2 planned to meet different people?

_____

3 was part of a coincidence involving his name?

_____

4 was physically hurt?

_____

b Listen and/or read again and circle the correct answer.

1 Why do people regret asking the writer about how he and his wife got together?
 a) He thinks it's boring.   **b)** It's really sad.

2 Where did Lynn and Andy actually meet for the first time?
 a) online   **b)** at a restaurant

3 Why did Lukas crash into Sofie's car?
 a) He wasn't looking where he was going.
 b) It was difficult to see where he was going.

4 What did Lukas think of Sofie when he first saw her?
 a) He thought she was beautiful.
 b) He thought she was OK.

5 What do Lukas and Sofie's and Nick and Susan's stories have in common?
 a) They both involved a crime.
 b) They both started with something bad happening.

6 When did Nick realise he really liked Susan?
 a) when he first met her   **b)** after a few weeks

7 When did the couple who met during jury service actually get together?
 a) during the trial   **b)** after the trial

8 What's Ben's dog's name?
 a) Ben   **b)** we don't know

The weird ways people meet

People always regret asking me and my wife how we got together. It's a long story, involving other relationships and several countries, and to be honest, it's not that interesting, so I'll spare you the details. We were at a restaurant in Tuscany on our summer holiday last year though, when we met another English couple who had a far more interesting story than us. Lynn and Andy had actually met online before they got together, or at least they thought they had. After a few casual conversations through an online dating agency, they decided to meet for real. Lynn arrived at the restaurant first, and shortly after was approached by Andy, who thought she was someone else. It turns out they'd both arranged to meet different people, but liked the look of each other, and that was that!

And they're not alone. It seems there are all sorts of places you might meet that special someone. Lukas met Sofie for the first time when he crashed into her car – on his bicycle. 'It was raining and I was coming downhill really fast, so I couldn't really see where I was going. Sofie opened her car door and I went straight into it, and off my bike.' explains Lukas, 'I was unconscious for a few seconds, and when I came round there was this beautiful young woman asking me 'Are you OK?' Well, after that, she went to the hospital with me and was just really kind, really caring, and we hit it off.'

Every cloud has a silver lining, so they say, and Nick McKiddie would most likely agree. He was leaving the office late one night when he got robbed by a group of young men. He wasn't hurt, but they stole his phone and wallet, so he called the police. Susan Harris, a young police officer at the time, attended the call. Nick explains, 'I don't know whether I was in shock because of what had happened, but I think it was love at first sight. I would never usually be so confident, but I just asked if she wanted to go for a drink sometime, and to my surprise, she said yes!' Nick and Susan got married last December.

It seems crime can indeed bring people together. I know a couple who started dating after doing jury service on a particularly lengthy court case. They were spending so much time together during the trial, that when it finally ended, they realised they were really missing each other!

Animals don't have the same social inhibitions as humans do, and this was certainly the case when Ri took her dog, Ben, to the local dog park. 'As soon as I took his lead off, he ran straight to another dog on the other side of the park, and started getting very friendly indeed' she laughs, 'I actually had to pull him away, and that was when I met Ben, the other dog's owner. We had a good laugh about it all, especially when we realised he had the same name as my dog. We became friends after that, and well, the rest is history.' ■

Vocabulary
Guessing the meaning of colloquial language

7 Replace the phrases in bold in the conversations with colloquial phrases from the box.

Alright   a rip off   A tenner
chill out   doing my head in
gonna   grab a coffee
How come   mate
totally stressed out   Wanna
was like   What's up

1 A: ᵃ **Hi**, Jess?

   B: Hey Carla. ᵇ **How are you**?

   A: ᶜ **Do you want to** ᵈ **have a coffee together**?

   B: Sorry, I can't right now. I'm ᵉ **going to** be late for class if I don't leave now.

2 A: Rrr! I'm ᶠ **feeling a little worried and not calm**!

   B: ᵍ **Why**?

   A: It's Leo, he's really ʰ **annoying me** at the moment. Last week at the café he ⁱ **said** 'Can you get the drinks? I'll pay you back tomorrow.' I haven't seen him since!

   B: Oh, ʲ **relax**, you know what he's like. He always says that but he's a good ᵏ **friend**, he'll pay you back in the end.

3 A: That'll be ten pounds, please.

   B: ˡ **Ten pounds**?? What ᵐ **an unreasonably expensive price**!

a *Alright* _____

b _____

c _____

d _____

e _____

f _____

g _____

h _____

i _____

j _____

k _____

l _____

m _____

Vocabulary
Idioms

8 Rearrange the words in the poem below to make idioms.

How to succeed at online dating

¹ ~~Out for eye an keep~~ *Keep an eye out for*
'charmers' who say that they're great;
The chances are they won't increase your heart rate.
Take what they say ² *salt a pinch with of*, _____
And if they lie then it's not your fault.
You don't need to ³ *truth with the economical be*, _____
Everyone knows you're a fountain of youth.
But if they've got beautiful, piercing eyes;
Then it's OK to ⁴ *lies little a few white tell*. _____
And if you take notice of all the above;
Who knows? You might ⁵ *in helplessly love fall*. _____

Language focus 2
More complex question forms

9 Use a word from A and a word from B to complete the questions.

A

how   what   which

B

benefits   expensive   far   ~~film~~   food   long
operating system   well

1 *Which film* do you want to watch at the cinema?

2 _____ _____ do you get on with your brother?

3 _____ _____ is your house from here?

4 _____ _____ do you have in your job?

5 _____ _____ does it take you to get ready to go out?

6 _____ _____ does your computer use?

7 _____ _____ couldn't you live without?

8 _____ _____ is it to fly first class?

10 Use the prompts to write questions with prepositions.

1 A: I'm really worried.

   B: *What / worried* *What are you worried about?*

2 A: Sshh! I'm on the phone!

   B: *Who / talk* _____ ?

3 A: I'd prefer to go by train, I'm afraid of flying.

   B: *What / frightened* _____ ?

4 A: I've got an interview for that job I told you about.

   B: Oh yeah? *Which one / apply* _____ ?

5 A: Hhmm, I wonder ...

   B: *What / think* _____ ?

6 A: I love playing online games.

   B: Really? *Who / play* _____ ?

11 Match a statement from A with a negative question from B. Add the negative auxiliary in B.

A

1 I'm never eating there again.   _b_
2 Oh dear, I'm going to get wet.   ___
3 Jill can't go in the sea on her own.   ___
4 Give me five minutes, then I'll be with you.   ___
5 Oh no! I've lost all my work!   ___
6 Liz isn't coming in to work today.   ___

B

a *Didn't* you like the restaurant?
b _____ she feeling well?
c _____ you have an umbrella?
d _____ you finished yet?
e _____ she swim?
f _____ you save it?

12 Rearrange the words to make indirect questions.

1 the / is / station / Do / know / you / bus / where ?
   Do you know where the bus station is?

2 her / if / I / present / liked / wonder / she
   _____

3 me / Tell / leave / time / want / to / you / what
   _____

4 you / the / from / tour / where / know / Do / guided / leaves ?
   _____

5 to / Can / up / get / remind / me / you / have / time / we / what / tomorrow?
   _____

6 party / They / going / whether / was / I / know / wanted / to / to / the
   _____

7 is / time / it / me / Can / tell / you / what ?
   _____

8 Do / costs / this / much / know / how / you ?
   _____

Pronunciation
Question intonation

13a 🎧 5.2 Listen to the sentences. Are they statements (S) or questions (Q)?

1 He said it was just a little white lie   _Q_
2 She's doing your head in   ___
3 They're hopelessly in love with each other   ___
4 His jokes didn't make me laugh   ___
5 She doesn't cry very often   ___
6 She hasn't had plastic surgery   ___
7 He's feeling really stressed out   ___
8 He spent the whole time dreaming about someone else   ___

b Listen again. Practise saying the questions.

Language live
Dealing with problems on the telephone

14a Rearrange the words to make responses, then use them to complete the conversations below. The first word of each response is underlined.

1 ~~good~~ / <u>When</u> / to / a / call / would / time / be / ?
2 message / earlier / my / Madrid / left / a / <u>I</u> / flight / about / to
3 up / <u>Sorry</u> / breaking / – you're
4 <u>I'll</u> / department / through / you / to / to / have / put / another
5 time / calling / <u>Sorry</u> / I / bad / am / a / at / ?
6 please / up / <u>Could</u> / bit / you / a / speak / ?
7 to / Jude / <u>thanks</u> / getting / me / for / back
8 with / bear / my / just / you'll / me / <u>If</u> / ask / I'll / boss
9 postcode / confirm / and / name / just / I / your / <u>Can</u> / ?
10 your / regarding / at / <u>it's</u> / son's / school / behaviour

a A: I'm sorry, Mr Grady is busy at the moment. Could you call back a bit later on?
   B: *When would be a good time to call?*
b A: Hello, Flight Centre, how can I help?
   B: Well, _____
c A: Patrick? It's Jude Cummins here – sorry it's a bit late.
   B: Oh, _____
d A: I'm calling about a mistake on my phone bill.
   B: Sorry to stop you there, _____

e A: Hello, this is Mrs Howard, Dan's mother – you wanted to speak to me.
   B: Yes, _____
f A: The only tickets we have left are at $15 for …
   B: _____
g A: The wedding menu? Now where did I put it? Should be here somewhere. Oops, now I've dropped everything and ….
   B: _____
h A: Could you check and see when my order was actually sent out?
   B: Sure. _____
i A: This is Shoreton's Wholesale Foods. Do you want to order anything this week?
   B: I'm not sure. _____
j A: We should have somebody with you by three o'clock.
   B: _____
   A: I said, we should have somebody with you by three.

b 🎧 5.3 Listen and check.

Writing
Types of message

15a Match informal phrases 1–7 with formal phrases a–g.

1 How's tricks?   _c_
2 V happy for u!   ___
3 By the way,   ___
4 OK   ___
5 Can't wait to see you!   ___
6 our treat   ___
7 Hey/Hi   ___

a suitable
b Dear
c I hope you are well.
d We will be willing to cover your expenses.
e Incidentally,
f I'm really looking forward to seeing you
g I'm really delighted for you.

b Read the three messages below. Which is

- informal?   ___
- semi-formal?   ___
- formal?   ___

A

○○○   New Message

Dear Mr Branhev

¹ I hope you are well. Please check the flight details below for your visit to London next week on 15th June for the planning meeting.

SUPERFLY AIRLINES

Outbound 15th June	Return 16th June
Flight No. SF6593	Flight No. SF6596
Depart:	Depart:
MUNICH MUC 06:50	LONDON LHR 10:15
Arrive:	Arrive:
LONDON LHR 09:45	MUNICH MUC 13:10

Can you confirm these flights are ²_____ ASAP?

On arrival, please take a taxi to head office and make sure you get a receipt.

Looking forward to seeing you again.

Best wishes

Vilma Rodrigues

B

○○○   New Message

³_____ Jan

Great to hear that you're heading over to London next week. How long has it been? Let's do something on Friday night after your meeting – ⁴_____ .

⁵_____ !

James and Charlie

C

○○○   New Message

Dear Leo

Congratulations on your engagement, ⁶_____ !
I've only just found out as I've been in London for the last two days on business.

I have to say that when I met Julia at the get-together last year, I thought she was really nice, and it was easy to see that you are right for each other.

⁷_____ , sorry I haven't been in touch for a long time, but things have been busy here. ⁸_____ at the wedding though, it will be a great chance to catch up with everyone!

⁹_____

Jan

---

c Complete the messages with phrases from exercise 15a.

d Write an appropriate message for each situation below.

○
- Send an email to an international colleague who is coming to your city for a meeting, explaining how to get to your office.
- Send an email to a friend who you are going to stay with, telling them about your plans and travel arrangements.

○
- Write a short note to your colleagues inviting them to a party you're having at the weekend.
- Write a note to a neighbour complaining about the rubbish in front of their house.

Listen and read
Greatest superheroes of all time

1 🎧 6.1 Listen to and/or read the article. Which of these superheroes are being described?

| Batman | The Incredible Hulk | Spiderman | Superman | Wonder Woman | Xena, Warrior Princess | The X-men |

Greatest Superheroes of all time

With their simple stories of good versus evil, comic-book superheroes are as popular today as when they first appeared. So, who are these much-loved characters?

Here is a brief introduction to four of the greatest superheroes of all.

1 _____
In 1939 America, DC Comics seized on the public's desire for escapism during a period of social and economic deprivation, and developed a new superhero. The creators of the 'Man of Steel' wanted a hero in a colourful costume who would look good in a comic book. Although there had been superheroes before, this was the first 'total package' with a costume, secret identity and abilities beyond those of mortal men. Born in a far-off galaxy, the baby hero discovers as he grows up that our sun gives him extraordinary powers: he can fly 'faster than a speeding bullet', has incredible strength and X-ray vision, and can only be hurt or destroyed by a green rock from his original planet, Krypton. He is adopted and brought up by Martha and Jonathan Kent to uphold truth, justice and the 'American way'. Whenever danger calls, he is never far from a telephone box and a quick change, ready to save the world. He's had several TV and film incarnations, the most successful of which starred Christopher Reeve and Margot Kidder in 1978. Ironically, creators Siegel and Shuster signed away their rights to the character for $130!

2 _____
Born on Paradise Island, youthful and immortal, this princess has been blessed by ancient gods and goddesses with powers of super strength and speed and the ability to fly. The superheroine made her first appearance in 1941. It is said she was invented by William Marston for DC Comics as a role model for girls and to raise the morale of US troops in World War II. Her alter-ego, Diana Price, works as a hospital nurse, but transforms herself by flicking her lasso. As well as the lie-detecting lasso, she has bracelets which can stop bullets, but unfortunately she loses her powers if she is tied up with her own lasso. She is instantly recognisable by her stars and stripes costume and in 1976, her adventures were brought to life in a three-year TV series starring ex-Miss USA Beauty Queen, Linda Carter.

3 _____
Created by artist Bob Kane and writer Bill Finger for DC Comics, the stories combined superheroics and a secret identity. This character cannot stop bullets, fly, or look through walls. He is a normal man who becomes one of the greatest crimefighters ever because of his detective skills, highly-trained physical abilities, amazing gadgets, and of course, his 'batmobile' car, kept in a hidden cave beneath his mansion. By day he is rich socialite Bruce Wayne, but at night he turns into 'the caped crusader', accompanied by his side-kick, Robin. He was memorably brought to life in the 1960s TV series and in the film of 1996, starring Michael Keaton, Kim Basinger and Jack Nicholson – a film that featured four of the series' best arch-villains: Catwoman, The Joker, The Penguin and The Riddler.

4 _____
Like many other superheroes, Peter Parker is an orphan, although he has an uncle (Ben) and aunt (Mae). Part of his appeal is that both adolescents and adults can readily identify with him. A poor school student, he goes on to become a regular working guy; a high-school teacher with both girlfriend and money problems. His world is turned upside down when his Uncle Ben is murdered. He gains his superpowers during a high school science demonstration when a radiated spider bites him and gives him superhuman strength and reflexes and the ability to stick to most surfaces. In the movie, which was the biggest money spinner of 2002, Parker grows webslingers which shoot and spin webs, and puts on his red and blue costume to fight arch-enemies such as the Green Goblin and Doctor Octopus.

2 Listen and/or read again and answer the questions.

1 How was Superman different from previous superheroes?

2 Where do his powers come from?

3 What is Superman's only weakness?

4 Who is Martha Kent?

5 Who gave Wonder Woman her powers?

6 Why was Wonder Woman created?

7 What is an 'alter-ego'?

8 What three things can Wonder Woman's lasso do?

9 In what important way is Batman different from the other three superheroes?

10 Who is Batman's alter-ego?

11 Who is his companion in crimefighting?

12 What happened to Peter Parker's parents?

13 Was he born with his superpowers?

14 What two things can he do which give him the name Spiderman?

Language focus 1
Perfect tenses

3 Choose the correct alternative.

1 I can't wait until July! I won't **have** / **have had** a break since Christmas, so I'll really **need** / **have needed** a holiday.

2 My New Year's resolutions are to go on a diet and to stop buying so many pairs of shoes! This time next year I'll **lose** / **have lost** weight and I'll **have** / **have had** more money to spend.

3 A: Here's the film – will the photos **be** / **have been** ready by Thursday?
B: Oh, I'm afraid we won't **do** / **have done** them by then – call in on Friday.

4 A: What's your decision on the takeover deal?
B: Can you give me until tomorrow? By then I'll **have** / **have had** more time to think about it and I'll **give** / **have given** you my decision.

5 Maria is doing a two-week lecture tour in Russia. When she gets back she'll **visit** / **have visited** ten cities and I'm sure she'll **feel** / **have felt** absolutely exhausted!

4 Use the prompts to write complete sentences, using the Present perfect.

1 I / have / lunch / that restaurant / every day / week.
I've had lunch at that restaurant every day this week.

2 you / finish / homework / yet?

3 I / never / try / Ethiopian food.

4 She / be / that school / January.

5 you / ever / read / any / Bukowski?

6 Many scientists / fear / we / already / pass / the tipping point / for climate change.

7 Good timing! I / just / make / fresh coffee.

8 Tratorie / score / 23 goals / far / season.

9 How long / it / be? I / not see / you / years!

10 What / you / do / today?

5 Complete the text with the Past perfect or Present simple form of the verb in brackets.

Goodbye, CEEFAX!

On 23rd October 2012, TV viewers in the UK ¹*said* [say] goodbye to a national institution: Ceefax, an information service which for nearly forty years ² _____ [provide] news, weather and even cheap holiday deals on pages which could be read by pressing a special button on your TV remote.

In a special ceremony, Olympic champion Dame Mary Peters ³ _____ it [switch off] at 23:32:19. By the end of 2012, all TVs ⁴ _____ [move] from an analogue to a digital service, and since Ceefax was also part of the analogue system, it ⁵ _____ [previously be] decided to switch it off as well.

Ceefax first ⁶ _____ [go] live in 1974. Researchers at the BBC ⁷ _____ [develop] it as a way of providing subtitles for deaf viewers, but it soon ⁸ _____ [become] a popular source of up-to-date information. Before the internet was commonplace, people ⁹ _____ [use] it to read the most recent and up-to-date news stories.

6 Match a sentence in A with a response in B. Complete each gap with the correct form of *have*.

A
1 Oh dear, I think I _'ve___ broken your MP3 player. _C_
2 You look slimmer than the last time I saw you. ___
3 Shall I phone back at three? ___
4 How long _____ you had your car? ___
5 When _____ finished dinner? ___
6 You were in a bad mood yesterday. ___
7 _____ you seen Mrs Jones this morning? ___
8 Here are your glasses. ___

B
a Yes, I _____ slept well the night before.
b Oh, thank you, I thought I _____ lost them.
c Let's have a look.
d Thanks, I _____ lost six kilos.
e No, she won't be in till this afternoon.
f For about five years, and it's still very reliable.
g Mm, the meeting _____ finished by then. Try at four.
h Probably by about eight-thirty, so you could phone then.

Vocabulary
Human achievements

7 For each sentence below, choose the option which is NOT possible.

1 He spent his lifetime *discovering* / *inventing* / *exploring* new planets.
2 She *won* / *defeated* / *led* the army in the famous battle of 1232.
3 Our campaign has *raised* / *donated* / *set* $50,000 this year. This money will help victims of the recent earthquake.
4 Her work inspired *others* / *speeches* / *future generations* to continue her research.
5 Morovia was *become* / *founded* / *led* by Addicius the Great.
6 The world record was *set* / *written* / *broken* in 2011.
7 The first 3D printers were *founded* / *invented* / *developed* in the 1980s.
8 In 2004, he *became* / *defeated* / *gave* the leader of the opposition.

8a Complete the gaps in the quiz with verbs from the box in the correct form.

b Do the quiz.

~~become~~ discover found give invent
set win write

QUIZ

1 In 1961, who _became_ the first man in space?

a Neil Armstrong
b Yuri Gagarin

2 Who _____ the World Wide Web in 1989?

a Bill Gates
b Sir Tim Berners-Lee

3 In 2012, who _____ a new world record for the highest skydive, at approximately 39km?

a Felix Baumgartner
b Usain Bolt

4 Which country _____ the most gold medals at the 2012 Olympics?

a USA
b China

5 Who was one of three people who _____ Apple Inc. in 1976, in order to sell the *Apple I* personal computer kit?

a Bill Gates
b Steve Jobs

6 Who _____ the classic novel *1984*?

a George Orwell
b Ernest Hemingway

7 Who _____ penicillin by mistake, after noticing a fungus growing on one of his/her experiments?

a Marie Curie
b Alexander Fleming

8 Who _____ great speeches on civil rights in the 1950s and 1960s, including a famous one which began, 'I have a dream…'?

a Martin Luther King, Jr.
b Richard Nixon

Writing
A summary

9a A TV company has asked for nominations for 'ordinary heroes' – people from your family or friends who have achieved something incredible. Read this summary and complete the gaps with the phrases in the box.

> ~~I'd like to nominate~~   As a result of his actions
> Eventually   He's one of the bravest ... people I know.
> In the 1960s   It's incredible to think that
> it took him years to   One

¹ *I'd like to nominate* my grandfather, Charlie, for the programme. ²_____ and hardest-working _____ .

³_____ , before my mother was born, my grandfather and grandmother were living in a poor area of London. My grandfather worked long hours in a factory earning very little, and ⁴_____ be able to afford to buy a modest place to live.

⁵_____ night, my grandmother became very ill and needed to go to hospital. Because they couldn't afford a car or any other transport, Charlie carried her all the way to the hospital, some five miles, wrapping her in his coat and rubbing her arms to keep her warm.

⁶_____ they reached the hospital and the doctors said she had arrived just in time, as she had a very low temperature and was close to death. Because Charlie had acted quickly and taken her to the hospital, he had saved her life.

⁷_____ , my grandmother recovered, and later gave birth to my mother.

⁸_____ because of his actions on that cold night, I'm here today to tell the story.

b Write your own nomination for someone in your family or one of your friends. Use the expressions from exercise 9a and think about the following things:

- the background to what they achieved
- what happened
- the effect it (has) had
- why you find it interesting/amazing.

Language focus 2
More about the Present perfect simple and continuous

10 Complete the gaps with the best form of the verb in brackets. Remember to use contractions.

A computer helpline

1 'I *'ve been working* (work) all morning on a document and _____ (only / manage) to print two pages of it.'

2 'I _____ (make) some back-up disks and I think I _____ (lose) one of my files.'

An English student

3 'I'm fed up. This is the third time I _____ (fail) the exam and I _____ (study) here for three years now.'

4 'I _____ (look) for an English–Polish dictionary in the library, but I _____ (only / find) a 1965 edition. The librarian said I should talk to you.'

A radio phone-in programme about health

5 'I feel terrible. I _____ (wake up) at 5 a.m. for the last month. I _____ (try) two different kinds of sleeping pill, but they just make me feel worse.'

6 'My husband _____ (behave) strangely recently. He _____ (start) talking to himself and he _____ (stop) going out with his friends. What do you think's wrong with him?'

11 Tick (✓) the sentences which are correct, and rewrite the sentences which are wrong.

1 Sue's been living with her parents recently. ✓

_____

2 I've been seeing this film before.
   I've seen this film before.

3 Since Richard was five, he's been collecting over a million football stickers.

_____

4 Be careful outside. It's snowed.

_____

5 I've been trying to fix this door handle all morning, and still have finished.

_____

6 Well done! You've fixed the problem with my computer!

_____

7 Where have you been? We've waited for nearly an hour!

_____

8 Do you mind if I leave early? I've finished the report you asked me to do.

_____

9 I've always been loving TV dramas.

_____

10 Do you think they're OK? They've been talking in there for ages.

_____

Pronunciation
Weak forms of auxiliary verbs

12a 🎧 **6.2 Listen and repeat.**

Have you
/həvjə/
Have you lived
Have you lived here long?
How long
How long have you been
_____ /həvjəbɪn/
How long have you been working here?

b 🎧 **6.3 Listen and write the questions.**

1 _What have you been doing?_ _____

2 _____

3 _____

4 _____

5 _____

6 _____

7 _____

8 _____

c Listen again and practise saying the questions.

Wordspot
first

13 Replace the words in bold with a phrase with _first_.

1 We travelled in **the best seats**.
   first class _____ (2 words)

2 **Initially** I found the job very difficult.
   _____ (2 words)

3 They fell in love **when they first saw each other**.
   _____ (3 words)

4 Carmen's **mother tongue** is Spanish.
   _____ (2 words)

5 I did a course in **giving simple medical help**.
   _____ (2 words)

6 **To start with** you need to stand with your skis parallel.
   _____ (3 words)

7 You can see Venus **very early** in the morning.
   _____ (2 words)

8 I'm afraid your **preferred** holiday dates are not available.
   _____ (2 words)

9 When I saw the apartment my **initial opinion** was very positive.
   _____ (2 words)

10 '... coming round the bend, Michael Schumacher is **leading**.'
   _____ (3 words)

Vocabulary
Celebrations and protests

1 Use the clues to find words related to celebrations and protests in the word square.

J	C	E	P	A	R	A	D	E	R	A	R	A	P
F	L	A	V	M	R	F	E	P	P	T	T	Y	L
M	A	R	C	H	E	R	M	Q	Q	A	C	W	A
G	P	A	Y	B	C	R	O	W	D	B	A	S	C
S	T	I	K	K	L	Y	N	S	Q	T	R	W	A
U	A	P	R	O	T	E	S	T	E	R	N	B	R
P	S	U	P	P	O	R	T	E	R	W	I	L	D
E	C	C	H	A	N	T	R	C	W	P	V	Q	T
W	H	L	B	A	W	B	A	B	A	U	A	K	C
S	E	A	M	F	Q	E	T	L	V	R	L	L	H
Z	R	S	R	L	S	I	I	N	E	Q	M	C	E
R	S	H	Y	A	D	R	O	M	B	A	R	T	E
T	Y	U	L	G	F	R	N	B	A	T	N	O	R

1 You do this by hitting your hands together continuously. c*lap*
2 When a group of people walk together to celebrate or protest something, they form a p___ .
3 A m___ is someone who walks with a group of people in a protest.
4 People join a d___ if they want to protest publicly about something.
5 A c___ is a large group of people in a public place.
6 A p___ takes part in a public activity to show their opposition to something.
7 You do this by repeating a word or phrase rhythmically. c___
8 A s___ is someone who publicly shows that they agree with something.
9 When two groups c___ , they fight in public.
10 Each country has its own f___ with a coloured pattern or picture on it.
11 You do this by moving your hand or arm from side to side. w___
12 If people go w___ , they behave in a very excited way.
13 At a c___ , there is dancing and a procession through the streets.
14 A p___ is a large notice which is posted or carried in a public place.
15 You do this by shouting to show your approval or support. c___

Language focus 1
Relative clauses

2a Look at the statements from a survey on 'pet hates'. Match a beginning in A with an ending in B.

A
1 I get really annoyed by cyclists *j*
2 I hate people ___
3 I hate jeans ___
4 I really don't like parties ___
5 I can't stand the taste of cola ___
6 I hate days ___
7 I really don't like restaurants ___
8 I get annoyed by children ___
9 I hate sandwiches ___
10 I hate politicians ___

B
a where I don't know anyone.
b whose policies change as soon as they get into power.
c whose parents let them make a lot of noise.
d where the service is slow.
e that are too tight.
f that have too much butter in them.
g who talk loudly on their mobile phones on the train.
h which has gone flat.
i when I don't get anything finished.
j who ride on the pavement.

b 🎧 7.1 **Listen and check.**

3a Read this summary of a short story called *The Model Millionaire* by Oscar Wilde.

Hughie Erskine, ¹<u>*who was a charming and attractive young man*</u>, was unfortunately not very successful in business and therefore did not have much money. He was in love with a beautiful girl called Laura Merton, ²_____ . One day, Hughie went to visit his friend, Alan Trevor, ³_____ . Trevor was just putting the finishing touches to a portrait of a beggar. The beggar, ⁴_____ looked sad and tired. 'Poor old man,' thought Hughie, 'he looks so miserable,' and gave the man a pound, ⁵_____ . The beggar smiled and said, 'Thank you, sir, thank you.' Hughie spent the rest of the day with Laura, ⁶_____ and he had to walk home because he had no money for a bus. The next day he went to a bar, ⁷_____ . Trevor told him that the 'beggar' was in reality Baron Hausberg, ⁸_____ . Hughie felt deeply embarrassed about giving him the pound. The following day, he received an envelope from the Baron, ⁹_____ . The message on the envelope said: 'A wedding present to Hughie and Laura from an old beggar'.

b Add this extra information in the gaps in the story, using non-defining relative clauses. Include commas where necessary.

- she was annoyed because he had given away his last pound
- his financial skills had made him a millionaire
- he was an artist
- ~~he was a charming and attractive young man~~
- it was all the money he had
- her father had demanded £10,000 to allow them to marry
- he was wearing torn, shabby old clothes and holding out his hat for money
- it had a cheque for £10,000 inside it
- he met Alan Trevor there

c 🎧 **7.2** Listen and check.

4 In these extracts from an online entertainment guide, join the sentences to make two longer ones, using relative pronouns.

CINEMA

Terminator 3: Rise of the Machines
🔞 109 min - Action | Sci-Fi | Thriller

Terminator 3: Rise of the Machines is the best of the *Terminator* series. It stars Arnold Schwarzenegger. This version is a 'must' for all Arnie fans. It includes new special effects.

1 *Terminator 3*, <u>*which stars Arnold Schwarzenegger, is the best of the Terminator series.*</u>
This version _____
_____
_____ .

COMEDY THEATRE

Stand-up, Character comedy
★ ★ ★ ★ ☆

The Comedy Collection finishes on Friday.

It features the brilliant Steve Jones and newcomer Martin Simons. Tickets are available on the door. They cost $18 and $30.

2 *The Comedy Collection* _____
_____
_____ .

CULTURE	ART & DESIGN	EXHIBITIONS

EXHIBITIONS   Top story

'*Old New York*' opens this weekend at the Brinkley Gallery. The Gallery has recently reopened. This exhibition of photographs takes you through fifty years of New York's history. It took six months to put together.

💬 19 comments

3 *Old New York* _____
_____
_____ .

A

Rod, Los Angeles

I was working as a journalist for a small, independent tech magazine at the time, and we had one invitation to the event – I was lucky enough to be chosen from our office to attend. The atmosphere as you entered the room was electric, everyone was excited and there was a constant buzz of chatter until the lights went out and the opening music came on. There had been rumours circulating as to what it was going to be for a few days, and so people already had a basic idea, but when it was finally revealed, I don't think anyone had expected to see something so well-designed – people were truly 'wowed', and there was an audible pause before everybody clapped and cheered. It was amazing to see just how far we'd come with technology at that point.

B

Clare, London

It was amazing. Everyone was already expecting something special because of who the director was, but this really surpassed our expectations. The fireworks were amazing, but what really topped it off was when the Queen arrived. At that point the crowd went wild, and people near me were waving a bright banner, which read: 'We love you London!' That summed it up for me, I think, as the whole show was a celebration of everything British. It was an excellent start to what turned out to be a fantastic event. The excitement lasted all summer.

C

Alvaro, Madrid

I was there with my brother, and we had been lucky enough to get tickets at the last minute. We hadn't really expected to get so far in the tournament, and had had to make lots of last-minute arrangements in order to be able to stay there for the match. But it was definitely worth it. Noone actually scored throughout the game, and we were literally on the edge of our seats the whole time. The atmosphere was a strange mix of excitement and exhaustion, as both players and spectators were getting tired. Then, Iniesta came through at the end of extra time and our half of the stadium went wild. It was crazy, people I didn't know were embracing me and shouting – several grown men were crying tears of happiness by the end. At that moment, I felt really proud of the team and my country. As this was the first time we'd won this competition, it really was quite an achievement.

D

Jess, Edinburgh

At the time I was probably one of the world's biggest fans of the series, so when I heard that I'd won a competition to be one of 1,700 people at a special event at the Natural History Museum, I couldn't believe my luck. This was a special gathering organised by the publisher, in which the author gave a speech, followed by an all-night event during which, at midnight, we all received a free, signed copy of the final book. There were so many unanswered questions from the earlier books in the series, which we were promised would finally be answered in this book. So, although the celebration was really good fun, to be honest, by the end of the night I just wanted to get home and start reading!

Listen and read
I was there!

5a 🎧 **7.3** Listen to and/or read the eyewitness accounts and match them to the events.

1 Spain winning the World Cup, 2010   _C_

2 The launch of the first iPad, 2010   ___

3 The launch of the final Harry Potter book, 2007 ___

4 The London Olympics Opening Ceremony, 2012 ___

b Are the statements below true (T) or false (F)?

1 Rod knew what was going to be revealed before the event.   _F_

2 He says people were impressed at the event.   ___

3 Rod thinks technology wasn't very advanced at that point.   ___

4 According to Clare, the event wasn't as good as people had expected.   ___

5 She says the best part of the event was when the Queen arrived.   ___

6 The banner Clare saw expressed the theme of the show for her.   ___

7 Alvaro had bought his ticket a long time before the game.   ___

8 He says the players were tired but the spectators were excited.   ___

9 Alvaro thinks the team achieved something significant.   ___

10 Jess felt lucky to have won the competition.   ___

11 The event finished at midnight.   ___

12 She didn't want to leave at the end of the night.   ___

Vocabulary
Special events

6a Match events 1–7 with sentences a–g.

1 Fair   _c_

2 Carnival   ___

3 Anniversary   ___

4 Music festival   ___

5 Wedding   ___

6 Funeral   ___

7 Public holiday   ___

a At the _reception_, the bride's father made a hilarious _____ in which he told lots of jokes about when he first met Jim.

b When the _____ act came on, the fans went wild and some of them tried to get on the _____ .

c The queues for the food _____ are long, but worth it! The food is amazing, and the children get free _____ .

d My favourite part was the 'Animals' _____ – the people on it were wearing special animal _____ and dancing as it went past the cheering crowds.

e The ceremony was beautiful, but when I saw the wooden _____ with flowers on it it was too much, and I cried, along with the other _____ there.

f To celebrate 50 years of marriage, my grandparents had a huge party, with beautiful decorations. They invited lots of _____ who brought them some wonderful _____ .

g In our town we do the same thing every year – a _____ through the town in the morning and a special meal in the afternoon, but the best thing is the colourful _____ display in the evening, when it's dark.

b Complete the sentences with the words in the box.

balloons	coffin	costumes	fireworks
float	guests	headline	mourners	parade
presents	~~reception~~	speech	stage	stalls

Language focus 2
Quantifiers

7 Correct the mistake in each sentence by crossing out or adding one word.

1 Has everyone got enough ~~of~~ food?

2 We know quite few of our neighbours, but not all of them.

3 We had a lot fun learning to scuba dive today.

4 I think we'll have a plenty of glasses for everyone.

5 There are a number reasons why the President resigned.

6 There was too much of food for four people to eat.

7 Over fifty people applied for the job, but a very few of them had the right qualifications.

8 There's a little of space for an extra chair here.

9 There are only a few of places where you can buy this type of cheese.

10 As any a doctor will tell you, you should eat a balanced diet.

8 Complete the gaps with quantifiers from the boxes below.

Rollerblades

The best ★★★★★
Racers
Super-fast and smooth, these skates come in ¹ _a number of_ different colours and have ² _____ extra features, including holes which give ³ _____ of ventilation. One small reservation is that there's ⁴ _____ noise when you go at high speed.

The worst ★
Grippers
These skates take ⁵ _____ time to put on – almost ten minutes – and don't provide ⁶ _____ support. They come in ⁷ _____ colours – only grey, black or white.

---

a number of   a great deal of   enough   plenty
quite a few   too much   very few

Choc 'n' Nut Ice cream

The best ★★★★★
Naughty and Nutty
This ice cream is full of flavour and should satisfy ⁸ _____ chocolate lovers. There are ⁹ _____ nuts and not ¹⁰ _____ sugar.

The worst ★
Nut and Choc
There are ¹¹ _____ nuts in this ice cream, but not many, and ¹² _____ chocolate. There is also ¹³ _____ sugar. A real disappointment.

---

any   plenty of   some   too much (x2)
very little

MP3 Players

The best ★★★★★
Genesis
We tried ¹⁴ _____ albums from pop to classical and ¹⁵ _____ kind of music sounded superb. There are only ¹⁶ _____ special features, but these are simple to use. The only problem is that ¹⁷ _____ shops actually have it in stock.

The worst ★
Horizon
We didn't think ¹⁸ _____ of the albums played well. It looks quite futuristic but there are ¹⁹ _____ buttons and flashing lights for our liking.

---

a few   a number of   any (x2)
too many   very few

Wordspot
take

9 Replace the words in bold with a phrase with *take* in the box in the correct form.

....

it takes   take after   take care of   ~~take off~~
take notes   take part   take place   take up

....

take off
y
1 You should **remove** all your jewellery before you go on a sunbed.
2 How long **is the journey** to get to the station?
3 Mrs Evans has offered to **look after** the cats while we're away.
4 I noticed that you **wrote information down** during the presentation.
5 I don't think **I'm like** anyone in my family.
6 Police reports say the accident **happened** just before midnight.
7 My sister's spent a lot of money on equipment since she **started** photography.
8 I'd love to **be involved** in a huge demonstration.

Writing
A review of an event

10a Read the review and match the topics in A with the information the reviewer gives in B. Complete the gaps in B where necessary.

A
1 the reason for going   _b_
2 how many people were there   ___
3 the atmosphere   ___
4 the reactions of the crowd   ___
5 the highlight(s)   ___
6 the negative(s)   ___
7 whether the reviewer would recommend it   ___

B
a they loved it
b had seen him on TV and was bought a ticket as a _____ present
c some of the jokes weren't _____
d _____ and friendly
e yes, even if you're not a big _____ of stand-up comedy
f a dance _____
g thousands

b Think of an event you have been to, e.g. a comedy show, a concert or a play. Make notes on the topics in exercise 10a, section A.

c Write a review of the event.

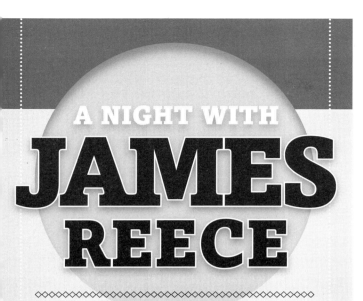

A NIGHT WITH JAMES REECE

I'm not normally a huge fan of stand-up comedy, but I had seen James Reece before on TV, so when my girlfriend bought me a ticket to his show for my birthday, I was actually quite looking forward to the show.

Thousands of people had turned up to see him perform, and the general mood of the crowd was relaxed and friendly – it seemed everyone was in a good mood and looking forward to a few laughs. The show started on time, and from the outset Reece was on top form. He opened with an anecdote about having recently had a baby, and then followed up with a few jokes about recent events in the news. The crowd loved it, applauding the carefully constructed jokes and cheering some of the funniest.

The highlight of the evening was when he did a dance routine, mocking a performer who had recently given a performance on national TV. It was so funny that I was in tears. The one thing I didn't like about the show though was that there were a few jokes I've heard him use before on TV, which was a bit of a shame as I'd expected the material to be new.

Overall though, I'd definitely recommend going to see him if you have the chance. Even if you're not a great fan of stand-up comedy, you'll love the show. What's more, you'll be quietly laughing to yourself for days after, as you keep remembering jokes from the show!

Language live
Awkward social situations

11 Rearrange the words to make responses, then match them with situations 1–5.

  a doesn't / slightest / It / the / matter / in
  b possibly / more / couldn't / any / I / manage
  c again / see / How / to / you / lovely
  d eat / I / afraid / prawns / can't / I'm
  e ~~love / able to / but / I'd / think / to come / I /~~
    ~~don't / be / I'll~~

1 Your great aunt invites you to a history lecture, which you are sure will be very boring.
I'd love to come, but I don't think I'll be able to.

2 Your girlfriend's mother offers you another piece of cake, but you don't really like it.
_____

3 At a dinner party the host offers you some prawns, but you are allergic to them.
_____

4 A woman comes up to you in a supermarket and tells you that you were at school together, but you don't remember her.
_____

5 Your friend is upset because her puppy chewed your bag while you were at her house having coffee.
_____

Pronunciation
Sounding polite

12a 🎧 7.4 Listen to some phrases said twice. Which one sounds more polite, A or B?

  1 I hope I didn't offend you. *A*
  2 How's everything going? ____
  3 Don't worry, it's not important. ____
  4 No, really. I couldn't manage any more. ____
  5 It doesn't matter. These things happen. ____
  6 I'll call you if I get a chance next week. ____

  b 🎧 7.5 Listen and practise saying the phrases with polite intonation.

08 STRANGE BUT TRUE

Vocabulary
Mysteries and oddities

1 Match the events with the headlines below.

1 a popular myth _c_
2 a miracle ___
3 a coincidence ___
4 a tragic incident ___
5 an unexplained natural phenomenon ___
6 a supernatural event ___
7 a hoax ___
8 a practical joke ___
9 a publicity stunt ___
10 a mysterious disappearance ___
11 an unfortunate mishap ___

a Falling baby saved twice ... by the same man

b Scientists unable to explain raining fish in honduras

c Great Wall of China not visible from space, new photos show

d 'Messages in bottles' discovered on beaches last week turn out to be advertisements

e 'UFO' photo not real, admits photographer

f Missing cruise ship 'cannot be explained' says coastguard

g Fire survivor says she was woken by ghost of late father

h Face of saint appears in sand in Italian seaside village

i TV channel shows 'documentary' on flying penguins on 1st April

j Footballer suffers sudden heart attack in cup final

k Bride slips and falls into lake while posing for wedding photos

Listen and read
Coincidences

2a 🎧 **8.1** Listen to and/or read these stories and match the pictures with the stories. There is one picture you do not need.

A

I work in a market in London, just at the weekends – I've got a second-hand book stall – and one day I was getting my stall ready when a lady came up and started looking at the books. She started chatting and
5 telling me how she used to live in that part of London and how much it had changed since she'd last been in the area. While we were talking, I put out a book and she picked it up. 'Oh, *Grimm's Fairy Tales*,' she said, 'I had a copy of this when I was a child. I used
10 to read it again and again.' She began flicking through it and I carried on laying out the books, and when I looked up she was just standing there shaking, and she'd gone completely white. 'But … but … this is my actual book,' she gasped, 'look, it's got my name, Joan,
15 in it. How on earth did you get it?' Then she told me how there'd been a terrible fire while her family were away on holiday, and the house had been burnt to the ground. She thought all her belongings had been destroyed. She pulled out her purse to buy the book
20 from me, but I stopped her. 'No, no … please accept it as a gift – it's such a wonderful story.'

B

I was walking along the road in Windsor where I live, when I heard a phone ringing in a phone box, and something prompted me to go in and pick it up. There was a voice at the other end saying, in a very
5 businesslike way, 'Sorry to bother you at home, Julian, but I can't find that file you were working on. Do you remember where you put it?' It was Jasmine, who I work with at my office in London. I stopped her before she could go on. 'Jasmine, I'm in a phone box – how
10 did you know I was here?' And she just said, 'Stop messing around, I'm really busy and I need that file.' I kept trying to convince her about where I was, but she just wouldn't believe me. Anyway, I told her where the file was, and then suddenly she interrupted me: 'Julian!
15 Hang on a minute, I didn't dial your home phone number! I dialled the Windsor code, but then I dialled your security card number, which is next to your name in the book at work.' So, somehow, my security card number just happened to be the same number as the
20 phone box that I was walking past.

C

A couple of years ago, we moved to an old house in the country and the man who lived there before had died, and we had to clear up a lot of his belongings. So we built a big bonfire at the end of the garden and took all the rubbish down there to burn. I'd just put
5 a box full of stuff onto the fire, and I was standing chatting, when there was a bang, and I felt something hit the side of my head. I took my earring off and there was a bullet stuck in it, which had been on the fire and had exploded. If I hadn't had the earrings on, it would've gone straight into my neck. And the scary thing was, the
10 bullet had the letter 'J' on it – and my name's Jane – so it was as if this bullet was intended for me!

1

3

2

4

b Listen and/or read again and match the sentences to the stories. There are four sentences for each story.

1 She must have felt astonished when she put the phone down. _B_

2 The previous owner must have had a gun in the house. ___

3 He could have walked on without stopping. ___

4 She could have missed him if she'd come on a Friday. ___

5 She can't have been standing very far away from the fire. ___

6 She can't be living in the area now. ___

7 She must have been delighted with what she found. ___

8 'J' might have been the initial of the manufacturer's name. ___

9 The fire can't have destroyed everything. ___

10 She could have been killed. ___

11 Somehow he must have known the call was for him. ___

12 She can't have been concentrating. ___

c Use words from the texts to complete these sentences. Try doing them without looking and then check your answers.

1 The man was getting his stall _ready_ when the lady came up.

2 She started to flick _____ a book.

3 He looked up and saw that she had _____ completely white.

4 Jasmine thought Julian was messing _____ at first.

5 She thought she had _____ his home number.

6 The number _____ to be the same number as the phone box.

7 The woman was clearing _____ the dead man's belongings.

8 She put a box full of _____ onto the bonfire.

9 She found a bullet _____ in the earring.

Language focus 1
Overview of modal verbs

3 Choose the correct alternative.

1 If you like, I **can** / **may** make an appointment for you to see Dr Krall tomorrow.

2 Passengers **mustn't** / **don't have to** smoke while on board the plane.

3 Don't let Sylvie climb that tree. She **can** / **might** fall.

4 You probably **shouldn't** / **mustn't** keep your passport in that pocket: it **should** / **could** easily be stolen.

5 I'm afraid Karen **can't** / **couldn't** come to the party tomorrow because she's got flu.

6 Oh no! It **mustn't** / **can't** be seven o'clock already! Jill and Graham will be here in 15 minutes!

7 I absolutely **ought to** / **have to** leave the house at six if I want to be at the station by six-thirty.

8 Be careful, that pot's very heavy. You **have to** / **could** hurt your back.

4 Replace the phrases in bold with a modal verb phrase. Sometimes there is more than one possible answer.

1 Is it true that cats **are able to** see in the dark? *can*

2 **It's necessary for you to** wear sunscreen when you go to the beach. _____

3 **It's impossible for it to** be that expensive. **I'm sure there's** a mistake. _____

4 Do you think **it's the right thing for me to** buy Alex a birthday present? _____

5 The doctor said **I'm not allowed to** lift anything heavy. _____

6 **It's possible that we'll** be a bit late tonight. _____

7 **It's not necessary for you to** join the team if you don't want to. _____

8 Frank's not in his office. I suppose **it's possible that he's** at lunch. _____

9 Come on, put those books away – **it's not a good idea for you to** be studying at this time of night. _____

10 **Am I allowed to** have tomorrow off? **It's necessary for me to** go to the dentist. _____

5 Complete the conversations with an appropriate modal verb. Sometimes there is more than one possible answer.

1 A: Is it possible to do colour copies on this printer?
   B: Well you _can_ , but it takes ages.

2 A: Do you think it'll snow tonight?
   B: It _____ . It's suddenly got very cold.

3 A: Don't you think you'd better see someone about your toothache?
   B: I know I _____ but I hate going to the dentist.

4 A: Isn't that your boyfriend over there with Susie?
   B: It _____ be! He's supposed to be in Paris on business!

5 A: Do I really need to speak Spanish for the job?
   B: Well, you _____ but it helps.

6 A: _____ I sit here?
   B: Sure, go ahead.

7 A: Come inside now – it's getting dark!
   B: Oh, _____ we? We're in the middle of a game.

Vocabulary
Extreme adjectives

6 Replace the words in bold with an extreme adjective in the box.

> deafening   exhausting   ~~furious~~   horrendous
> huge   ridiculous   starving   stunning
> superb   tiny

● ○ ○

furious
                y
There were ¹ **very angry** scenes in Parliament today when the government's transport plans came under attack. 'The proposed law is ²**very silly** and just shows how out of touch the government is with the country,' said the Shadow Transport Minister

---

³**Very big** crowds greeted a rare open-air performance by the Manchester Philharmonic last night. After nearly an hour's delay, the orchestra came on to ⁴**very noisy** applause, and went on to give what many have described as a ⁵**very good** performance.

● ○ ○

Dear all,

Arrived here after an ⁶**very tiring** two day drive through France. Staying in a ⁷**very small** village with ⁸**very beautiful** views across the mountains. Hotel food is ⁹**very bad**, and we were ¹⁰**very hungry** until we found a lovely little restaurant nearby …

7a Four of the sentences below are wrong. Correct the mistakes by changing the word in bold.

1 Wear a coat when you go out – it's **quite** cold for this time of year. ✓
2 I find the idea of bungee jumping **absolutely** frightening. _____
3 Catherine was **very** furious about the mess that the children had made. _____
4 Can you turn your music down, please? It's very **noisy**. _____
5 We've been moving house all day – we're absolutely **exhausted**. _____
6 Mum, I'm absolutely **hungry** – can I have a burger? _____
7 Have you seen the new sitcom on ABC? It's **really** funny. _____
8 Didn't you take an umbrella? You must be absolutely **wet**. _____

b 🎧 8.2 Listen and check.

Language focus 2
Past modals

8a Cross out the modals which do not fit in the sentences below. Sometimes you only need to cross out one.

1 Look, the river's frozen! It ***must have been*** / ~~***should have been***~~ / ~~***can't have been***~~ very cold during the night.
2 A: I think Greg's out. He didn't answer the phone.
    B: But he ***might not have heard*** / ***couldn't hear*** / ***may have heard*** it – he sometimes plays his music very loud.
3 A: Here, I brought you some flowers.
    B: Oh, you ***shouldn't have done*** / ***didn't have to do*** / ***couldn't have done*** that.
4 Sally! Look where you're going when you cross the road. You ***must have been*** / ***could have been*** / ***might have been*** hit by a car!
5 At school we ***could learn*** / ***had to learn*** / ***managed to learn*** two languages if we wanted to.
6 A: I'm very sorry I'm late, I got stuck in traffic.
    B: Well you ***could have called*** / ***must have called*** / ***should have called*** to let us know. We've been waiting for half an hour.
    A: I was going to phone, but I ***couldn't find*** / ***can't have found*** / ***couldn't have found*** the number.

b 🎧 8.3 Listen and check.

9 Use the prompts to write complete sentences.

A
PETE: Oh no! I / lose / my wallet.
Oh no! I've lost my wallet.

SUE: Where / last / have it?
1 _____
_____

PETE: I / not know. I / use / last night when I / buy / train ticket so I / must / have it then.
2 _____
_____

SUE: you / use it / since then?
3 _____
_____

PETE: No. I suppose / might / lose it on / train or / I might / leave it / home this morning.
4 _____
_____

SUE: Why / you / phone home / check?
5 _____
_____

B
STEVE: Where / you / be? / It / be / eleven o'clock!
1 _____
_____

ZENA: I / get / stuck / traffic.
2 _____
_____

STEVE: Well, you / should / phone!
3 _____
_____

ZENA: I / be / sorry, I / leave / mobile phone / home.
4 _____
_____

STEVE: But if I / know / you / be / late / I could / go / pub.
5 _____
_____

ZENA: I / be / really sorry.
6 _____
_____

10 Vanessa, Georgina, Mike and Gavin are students who share a house. Complete the gaps with the positive or negative past form of a modal verb (*should, ought to, must, can't, might,* or *could*) and an appropriate verb.

VANESSA: Someone forgot to lock the front door last night.

MIKE: Well, it ¹ *can't have been* me. I definitely remember locking it, so it ²_____ someone who came home after me.

GEORGINA: You slept in the garden all night! Why didn't you wake us up?

GAVIN: Well, I rang the bell for ages, but no one answered. You ³_____ to bed.

GEORGINA: Oh, you idiot. You ⁴_____ a stone at the window.

GEORGINA: Vanessa and Gavin aren't speaking to each other this morning.

MIKE: They ⁵_____ an argument. I remember hearing shouting last night.

VANESSA: Who's this?

MIKE: It's just my friend, Bill.

VANESSA: Well, you ⁶_____ us that you were bringing someone home. I just sat on him!

GEORGINA: Oh no! Where have my chocolates gone? There are only two left!

VANESSA: Well, I think the cat ⁷_____ them because I forgot to feed him, or it ⁸_____ Gavin, because you know what he's like when he's hungry!

GAVIN: Look at this – and Georgina still hasn't done the washing-up!

MIKE: Well she ⁹_____ the note.

MIKE: You look terrible.

GAVIN: Yes, I feel really sick.

MIKE: Well, you ¹⁰_____ Georgina's chocolates. It's your own fault.

Pronunciation
Weak form of *have*

11a 🎧 8.4 **Listen to the pairs of sentences and circle the one you hear.**

1 **a** She can't have sent the letter.
  b She can't send the letter.
2 **a** It must have cost a fortune!
  b It must cost a fortune!
3 **a** You should have become an actor.
  b You should become an actor.
4 **a** Careful, she might have hit you.
  b Careful, she might hit you.
5 **a** It could have hurt a bit.
  b It could hurt a bit.
6 **a** We can't have put it in the wrong place.
  b We can't put it in the wrong place.

b 🎧 8.5 **Listen and practise saying the phrases with the weak form of *have*.**

Vocabulary
Mysteries

12 **Put the letters in the correct order to complete the sentences.**

1 It's a film about **sagterngs** who controlled the illegal alcohol trade during the prohibition period in the USA. *gangsters*
2 The neighbour said she'd heard **arcsmes** coming from the apartment. _____
3 This castle was built as a **sterfros** to protect the young king in the event of an invasion. _____
4 Do you believe there are **slinea** out there on another planet? _____
5 The 'photo' of a **FOU** turned out to be a hoax. _____
6 One of the patients was brought in with **stonghu dwosun**, where she'd been shot several times. _____
7 Carl stuck to his story, but he failed the **eli trocteed** test. _____
8 When she arrived in the country, she was immediately charged with **cadbintou** of the missing child. _____
9 Preparing for the approaching hurricane, the doors had to be **leadin thus**. _____
10 Cars of the future won't need wheels – they'll **rovhe** over any surface. _____

Writing
A story

13a **Complete the table with the words in the box.**

alone ~~amazing~~ awful bolts carriage
coincidence cold dark, empty road
deafening frightened golden disc hoax
huge incredible iron bars key massive
practical joke prescription for medicine quiet
ship small box stormy stunning
supernatural event tiny tired
unexplained natural phenomenon unfortunate mishap

Adjectives	Mysteries and oddities	Objects/places
amazing		

b **Complete the sentences below to write a story about a mystery. Use the vocabulary from exercise 13a and your own ideas.**

It happened to me ...

This supernatural event (mystery/oddity) happened to me on a _____ (adjective) night when I was in/on/at _____ (place), on my way to _____ (name of city/town/etc.).

I'd been _____ (verb) as normal, and was feeling a bit _____ (adjective) when suddenly a(n) _____ (object) appeared in front of me. I _____ (verb). As I got a closer look, I could see it was _____ (adjective) and making a (n) _____ (adjective) sound.

What I couldn't understand was how/why/where _____ (what?). Was this a(n) _____ (mystery/oddity), or just a (n) _____ ?

Then, just as quickly as it had appeared, it disappeared, and I was left with _____ (object). I decided to _____ (what?).

Five days later, I arrived in _____ (place). I told everyone there what had happened, but nobody would believe me. It was then that I remembered the _____ (object), so I took it out to show it to everybody. But when I pulled it out, to my horror, I saw it had _____ (what?).

To this day nobody really knows if it was a(n) _____ (mystery/oddity) or a _____ (mystery/oddity) that happened to me that night.

Listen and read

How to ...

1a 🎧 **9.1** Listen to and/or read the stories. Choose the best heading for each one.

How to:
- invest money successfully
- get the attention of the police
- get a table at a restaurant
- prevent a burglary
- make money
- reserve a table at a restaurant

A

How to _____

A young man asked a rich old man how he had become wealthy. The old man said, 'Well, son, it was 1932 in the depth of the Great Depression. I was down to my last cent. I invested that cent in a golf ball. I spent the day polishing the golf ball and at the end of the day I sold it for two cents. The next morning, I invested that two cents in two golf balls. I spent the entire day polishing them and sold them for four cents. I continued like this for a few weeks and by the end of that time I'd accumulated a hundred dollars. Then my wife's father died and left us three million dollars.'

B

How to _____

Stewart Montgomery of Glasgow, Scotland was going to bed one night when his wife peered out of the bedroom window and told him he'd left the light on in the garage. Montgomery opened the back door to go and switch off the light but saw that there were two men moving about in the garage. He phoned the police, who asked, 'Is there actually a burglar in your house?' When he said no, they told him to lock all his doors and stay inside; noone was free at the moment but someone would come when available. Montgomery hung up, waited a minute, and then phoned back. 'Hello. I just called to tell you that there were burglars in my garage. Well, you don't have to worry about them now because I've just shot them both.' Within two minutes, four police cars and an ambulance screeched to a halt outside his house. At least ten police officers rushed into the garage and caught the men red-handed. One of the policemen said to Stewart, 'I thought you said you'd shot them!' 'I thought you said there was noone available!' replied Montgomery.

C

How to _____

A couple went into an exclusive restaurant in Los Angeles. 'I'm sorry,' said the head waiter, 'there are no tables available.'
'Do you know who I am?' said the man. 'I am Dwayne Wright, the film director.'
'I'd like to help you, Mr Wright, but there are no tables left tonight.'
'I'm certain that if the President came in and asked for a table, there would be one free.'
'Well, I suppose so, ... yes,' said the waiter after a brief pause. 'Yes, there would be a table for the President.'
'Good. I'll take it. The President isn't coming this evening, so I'll have his table!'

b Listen and/or read again. Who ...

1 inherited something?
   The rich old man and his wife
2 was polite but firm? _____
3 lied? _____
4 was hesitant? _____
5 was diligent and hardworking?
   _____
6 was persuasive? _____

c Replace the words in bold with a word or phrase from the stories. The letter in brackets shows in which story you will find the word or phrase.

1 They were very **rich** and lived in a beautiful mansion. (A) *wealthy* _____
2 Things were pretty bad: I'd lost my job and my home, and I **hardly had any money left**. (A) _____
3 Over the years, we've **steadily collected** an enormous number of books. (A) _____
4 She **looked carefully** round the door, hoping he'd gone. (B) _____
5 After I'd **put the phone down**, I regretted being so rude to her. (B) _____
6 He saw the red traffic light at the last minute and **stopped suddenly with a terrible noise**. (B) _____
7 The police arrived at the bank and caught the robber **in the act of committing a crime**. (B) _____
8 There was a **short silence** and then the audience broke into deafening applause. (C) _____

d 🎧 **9.2** Listen and check.

Vocabulary

Phrasal verbs

2 Use a verb from box A in the correct form and a particle from box B to complete the sentences.

A

look   make   ~~pass~~   see   stand (x2)

B

~~out~~ (x2)   through   up (x3)

1 The room was so hot and crowded, I could hardly breathe and nearly *passed out*.
2 I've always _____ to my father, because he always put our interests first when we were growing up.
3 The Prime Minister tried to pretend he was 'cool' by playing the guitar, but everyone _____ the act immediately.
4 You'll need to _____ from the crowd if you want to get noticed.
5 You shouldn't let them push you around like that. You need to _____ for yourself.
6 Karen's such a bad liar that whenever she makes an excuse, you can easily tell if she's _____ it _____ .

Language focus 1

Use and non-use of articles

3 Put five indefinite articles (*a/an*) and five definite articles (*the*) in the correct places in the joke.

> An
> y
> old man was backing BMW into parking space when bright red sports car drove in behind him and took space. Young man jumped out and said, 'Sorry, old man, but you've got to be young and fast to do that.' Old man ignored young man and kept reversing until BMW had destroyed sports car completely. 'Sorry, son, you've got to be old and rich to do that!'

4 Complete the pairs of sentences with a word from the box, then insert *the* where necessary.

exercise   music   people   poetry   ~~traffic~~

1 a *Traffic* is a big problem in our cities.
  b Sorry we're so late. _____ on the way here was really bad.
2 a I was doing _____ you showed me for twenty minutes yesterday and it made my legs ache!
  b _____ is really good for you.
3 a I hate _____ who chew gum all the time.
  b I thought _____ at the next table were very rude to the waiter.
4 a Janet doesn't like listening to _____ when she works.
  b _____ they play on Radio 5 is terrible.
5 a _____ of Dante is very passionate.
  b We studied _____ at school, but I haven't read much since.

5 Complete the gaps in the holiday advertisement with *the* where necessary.

WINTER BREAKS WITH

SUNSPOT HOLIDAYS

Visit ¹*Australia*!

Spend the first three days in ²_____ Sydney.

See ³_____ Sydney Harbour Bridge.

Go shopping in ⁴_____ George Street.

Visit ⁵_____ Blue Mountains, just outside the city.

Then go north to ⁶_____ Whitsunday Islands and practise your diving in ⁷_____ Pacific Ocean.

Finally, see the crocodiles from the film *Crocodile Dundee* in ⁸_____ Kakadu National Park.

This is a once in a lifetime offer!

Fourteen days that you'll never forget.

CALL 010 600 4000 NOW

6 Cross out *the* or *a* in the sentences below if they are unnecessary. Tick the correct sentences.

1 **a** Nelson Mandela spent many years in ~~the~~ prison.
  b The prison was a long way from June's house, so she couldn't visit her husband very often.
2 **a** I cycle past the hospital every morning on my way to work.
  b My sister has been in a hospital since her operation.
3 **a** Billy's still at the school; his lessons don't finish until four o'clock.
  b Elena works at the local school as a teaching assistant.
4 **a** I waited in the church for the rain to stop.
  b We go to the church every Sunday for the ten-thirty service.
5 **a** I left the university when I was twenty-one.
  b My parents only visited the university once, on my graduation day.

7 Complete the gaps in the extracts with *a*, *an*, *the* or no article (–).

Flying problems

Nearly all [1] _____ air travellers suffer from [2] _____ jet lag to some extent. In [3] _____ recent survey, only five per cent said they had never had [4] _____ problem. [5] _____ most common complaints were [6] _____ tiredness and [7] _____ disturbed sleep for up to five days after flying.

Here are some tips to help:
- try to book [8] _____ morning flight;
- avoid [9] _____ alcohol and drink plenty of [10] _____ still water;
- get up and walk around [11] _____ plane regularly;
- when you get to your destination, try not to sleep during [12] _____ next day and go outside as much as possible.

Depression

[13] _____ Canadian study may help to explain why [14] _____ women are more likely to suffer from [15] _____ depression and [16] _____ eating problems than [17] _____ men. [18] _____ Canadian study shows that [19] _____ women's brains produce around 37 per cent less serotonin, [20] _____ important factor in many key brain functions, including [21] _____ regulation of [22] _____ mood and appetite.

8 Read these tips from a magazine about finding a good fitness club. Six of the lines are correct and seven have an unnecessary article. Tick (✓) the correct lines. Circle the unnecessary articles (*a/an/the*).

1 (The) many people go to a gym regularly, to try to
2 lose the weight and cope with the stress of modern life.
3 Here are the some tips for finding the best gym for you.
4 Visit at least three clubs at the time of day you plan to work out.
5 Check for the cleanliness, especially in the changing rooms.
6 Ensure the equipment is well maintained and suited to your
7 requirements. Expect the well-qualified, presentable instructors.
8 Check that an instructor is available in the gym area at all times
9 for an assistance. Is the club security-conscious – do you need
10 an ID card to get in? Do you need to pay a membership fee and
11 does the fee include the cost of aerobics classes? Choose a gym
12 a short distance away – if it takes you more than the thirty minutes
13 to get there, you probably won't go.

9 Use the prompts to write full sentences, paying attention to the use of articles.

1 At / Christmas / my mother usually / go / to / church at eight o'clock, then she / come / home and / cook / huge lunch.

_____
_____
_____

2 Deborah / leave / home / last year – now she / work / as / lecturer in / Vancouver.

_____
_____
_____

3 I / visit / Uncle Frank in / hospital / yesterday morning. He / be / very lucky, because he / have / got one of / best heart specialists in / UK.

_____
_____
_____

4 A: Be / Jamie happy at / school?
B: Yes. He / like / teachers, and / school / be only / five minutes away, in / Kilmorie Road.

_____
_____
_____

5 Gordon / be / terrible cook. He / invite / us for / dinner / last Saturday evening and it / be / one of / worst meals / I / ever / have.

_____
_____
_____

Language focus 2
Different ways of giving emphasis

10a Make this soap opera script more dramatic by inserting the words in the box. *The words are in the correct order.*

~~so~~	on earth	completely	far too
really do	absolutely	far too	absolutely

Drew enters the flat, to see Jenny looking very upset. The noise of plates smashing and screaming can be heard coming from the kitchen.

so
↓
JENNY: Oh Drew, I'm pleased to see you …

DREW: Why? What's all that shouting in the kitchen?

JENNY: It's Simon – he's gone mad, because he thinks Anna's seeing someone else.

DREW: *(walking towards the kitchen)* Right, I'm going to stop this …

JENNY: *(running after him and pulling him back)* No, it's dangerous! He's got a knife!

DREW: You don't think he'll use it, do you?

JENNY: I think he might, because he's been drinking … Anna's terrified.

DREW: *(walking around agitatedly)* This is ridiculous … let's try and talk to him.

JENNY: It won't do any good, he's drunk.

DREW: *(picking up the phone)* OK then, let's call the police – there's nothing else we can do.

b 🎧 **9.3 Listen and check.**

Anna and Simon; Jenny and Drew.

11 Rearrange the words to make sentences with emphasis.

1 his / like / What / humour / is / most / I / of / sense .

What I like most is his sense of humour.

2 like / does / Susan / you, / bit / a / just / shy / she's .
_____

3 a / be / Don't / baby / such !
_____

4 you / earth / Where / been / have / on ?
_____

5 absolutely / party / Jamie's / fantastic / was .
_____

6 Thomas / know / does / he / wants / get / to / how / what !
_____

7 horrendous / traffic / always / completely / is / The / route / that / on .
_____

8 film / asleep / It / such / a / was / end / before / boring / fell / that / I / the .
_____

9 Jenny / jacket, / me / who / was / borrowed / not / It / your .
_____

10 earth / Why / her / say / that / on / would / you / to ?
_____

Pronunciation
Sentence stress for giving emphasis

12a Which of the underlined words in each sentence below is especially stressed? Circle the correct option.

1 Wow, you look (absolutely) stunning!
2 What on earth have you two been up to in here?
3 It was Sheila who said those things about you, not me.
4 You're such a lucky guy!
5 I did leave a message for you – you must just have missed it.
6 Who on earth can we find to do it at such short notice?
7 It's going to be far too expensive to hire a band for the wedding.
8 What annoyed me was that he didn't once say 'thank you'.

b 🎧9.4 Listen and check. Practise saying the sentences with the correct stress.

Wordspot
right and *wrong*

13a Put the word *right* or *wrong* into these sentences. Then match 1–10 with a–j to make conversations. The conversations begin with the phrase from a–j.

1 That's all `right` by me, I'm in no hurry.   _g_
2 Let me have a look … no, there's nothing with it, it just needs cleaning.   ___
3 The green one, I think. Yeah, that looks about.   ___
4 Don't worry, I'll be back.   ___
5 It's not like you to stay in on a Saturday night. What's?   ___
6 No, you've got it on the way round.   ___
7 Well, it serves you for spreading gossip about her in the first place.   ___
8 Yes, I must admit I was completely about him.   ___
9 No, we need to do it here, right now.   ___
10 It seems everything's gone for him lately; he lost his job and he's split up with his girlfriend.   ___

a Which hole does this part fit into?
b Is this skirt supposed to have pockets at the front?
c Why is Dave so depressed at the moment?
d I think I'll just stay in and watch TV.
e I don't think this mouse is working properly.
f Let's leave it until later.
g Do you mind if we stop at the shop quickly on the way?
h Wait, where are you going?
i Gary's really quite interesting when you get to know him, isn't he?
j I can't believe Justyna just spoke to me like that in front of everyone else.

b 🎧9.5 Listen and check.

Language live
Suggestions and advice

14a Complete the conversations with the words in the box.

advice	'd	definitely	hadn't	important
mean	~~not~~	perhaps	should	speaking
suggest	~~suggestions~~	thought	ought	
were	would			

1 A: Any _suggestions_?
   B: Why _not_ give them a call?
2 A: Have you ever _____ about writing your own book?
   B: That's a really good idea, I _____ thought of that.
3 A: This TV hasn't worked properly since I bought it.
   B: If I _____ you, I _____ take it back.
4 A: I just wondered if you've got any advice about what I _____ do?
   B: To be honest, the most _____ thing is to do what's right.
5 A: You should _____ ask her about it, she might just have forgotten.
   B: Yeah, _____ you're right.
6 A: Grant can't decide what he wants to do when he leaves school.
   B: I _____ recommend _____ to a careers counsellor.
7 A: Hello, I'd like some _____ about these smart phones, please.
   B: Yes, of course. First things first, I would _____ that you decide which features you want.
8 A: You _____ to have a word with your boss about your hours, you know.
   B: I know what you _____ , it's just hard to find the right time.

b 🎧 **9.6** Listen and check.

Writing
A speculative covering letter

15a Read the speculative cover letter below and choose the correct options.

From: Flori Aish

To: code up

Subject: Proposal for new app

Dear [1](**Sir/Madam**)/ **Sirs**

My name is Flori Aish and I am writing to [2]**know** / **enquire** whether you are looking to take on any new ideas for smart phone apps.

I have recently developed an app aimed at the health and fitness sector which makes recommendations for your daily life based on physical measurements taken by your phone. The app is [3]**currently** / **right now** in beta stage and I am hoping to develop it further after securing development funds.

I am an IT teacher at Newford Park High School, but in my spare time I create apps and am [4]**looking** / **wanting** to start a new career as an app developer. With [5]**its** / **it's** excellent reputation in app development, Codeup Design is [6]**exactly the type** / **the type exactly** of company I would like to publish my idea.

A full proposal and technical specifications are [7]**attached** / **enclosed**, and I would be [8]**greatful** / **grateful** if you [9]**would consider** / **to consider** my app for further development. Please get in touch if you [10]**are wanting** / **require** any further information.

I look forward to [11]**hearing** / **hear** from you soon.

Yours [12]**sincerely** / **faithfully**

Flori Aish

b Choose one of the ideas below (or your own idea), and write a speculative cover letter to promote it.

- An app you would like to get developed.
- An idea for a computer/video game you would like to develop.
- A book or film you would like to write.
- An invention you would like to develop.

10 MEDIA

Vocabulary
The media

1 Complete the grid using the definitions below.

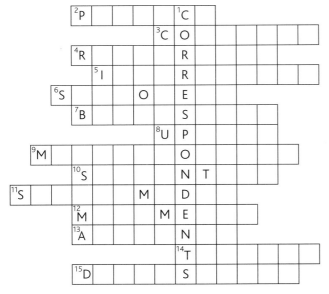

1 Foreign _____ : journalists who report news from abroad.

2 _____ placement: a type of advertising where a company arranges for its product to be placed in a TV programme or film.

3 The amount of space a newspaper devotes to a topic.

4 The number of people who read a newspaper.

5 A type of media that you can communicate with.

6 A TV programme about the daily lives of a group of people, which is shown regularly.

7 A newspaper printed on large sheets of paper, usually serious in style.

8 To transfer a file from your computer to the internet.

9 A way of sharing your experiences with others on the internet, in a limited space.

10 The amount of time people spend in front of a TV, computer or tablet.

11 Websites where you can share links and files with friends and communicate with them.

12 Media which reach large numbers of people.

13 Target _____ : the group of people a TV programme is aimed at.

14 A newspaper which isn't serious and has lots of photos and stories about celebrities.

15 A fictional, serious story shown on TV in episodes.

Listen and read
Where's the soap?

2a 🎧 **10.1** Listen to and/or read the article. Which of the following things are mentioned?

1 How TV programmes aren't always what you expect.

2 The number of soap operas on TV today.

3 The history of soap operas.

4 Where the name 'soap opera' comes from.

5 Some famous actors in soap operas.

6 Differences in soap operas around the world.

7 The future of soap operas.

8 Types of storylines.

9 Some strange examples of stories.

10 The author's favourite soap opera.

b Listen and/or read again. Are these statements true (T) or false (F), according to the article?

1 The author doesn't always see what he expects to see on TV. ____

2 The first soap opera was produced by a woman who used to be a teacher. ____

3 Ninety percent of all radio programmes in 1940 were soap operas. ____

4 Companies which made cleaning products sometimes produced soap operas. ____

5 A 'cliffhanger' is a story which never ends. ____

6 Some soap operas have been around since the 1950s. ____

7 In Latin America, soap operas are called *telenovelas*. ____

8 In the UK and Australia, characters come from rich backgrounds. ____

9 Romance is more typical of paperback novels than soap operas. ____

10 One soap opera showed a dog dreaming in one episode. ____

Where's the soap?

It's funny how TV programmes don't always live up to your expectations. I can't tell you how many times I've turned on the 'news', only to be told who the winner of a talent show is or what a celebrity has been wearing. Or the number of 'comedies' which didn't make me laugh. So it comes as no surprise that rarely does a 'soap opera' contain soap or singing, let alone classical singing. So, where is the soap?

In 1930, the manager of a Chicago radio station approached a detergent company in order to get sponsorship for a daily, fifteen-minute drama about a woman who left her job as a speech teacher to work in radio. This was to become *Painted Dreams*, a serial considered to be the first soap opera. The format was so popular that by 1940, radio soap operas made up 90% of commercially sponsored daytime radio. The word 'soap' comes

from the fact that these programmes were sponsored (and sometimes even produced) by companies which produced domestic cleaning products. They were aimed at housewives, who at that time would be at home.

All soap operas are defined by the fact that their storylines are continuous. Several plots often run at the same time, and each episode usually ends with a 'cliffhanger', an open ending designed to make people want to watch or listen to the next episode. Most soap operas are 'open', in that they never end. Some British soap operas have been on TV since the 1950s, though obviously the characters come and go. However, in Latin America, soap operas tend to be 'closed'. Although they last for months and can have hundreds of episodes, *telenovelas* (as they're called there) do reach a conclusion.

In the Americas, soap operas tend to focus on glamorous and seductive characters with wealthy lifestyles, whereas in the UK and Australia, they tend to be based on the lives of working class people. In both cases, storylines are based around family life, relationships, moral issues and sometimes topical issues. Romance and secret relationships feature heavily, and these can be compared to those of old style paperback romance novels. Plots can often move into bizarre areas, such as in an episode of US soap *Dallas*, where in order to bring back a 'dead' character, it was shown that a previous season had all been a dream of one of the characters. Perhaps not as strange as an Australian soap which had one scene showing a male dog dreaming about the female dog from next door!

Language focus 1
Reporting people's exact words

3a Tick the comments below that are compliments.

1 Michael told me that I've got beautiful eyes. ✓
2 Julie said that she admired my honesty. ___
3 Maddy said that I had cheated in the exam. ___
4 Carrie said that she wants to get her hair cut like mine. ___
5 Marcia and Paul said they wouldn't be late. ___
6 Tom said I looked as if I'd lost weight. ___
7 My boss told me that he was going to reduce my salary. ___
8 Tina said it was a long time since she'd eaten such delicious food. ___

b Write the people's exact words in exercise *a*.

1 *You've got beautiful eyes.* _____
2 _____
3 _____
4 _____
5 _____
6 _____
7 _____
8 _____

4 Complete the conversations, using information from the speech bubbles.

1 A: Why are you wearing a raincoat?
B: They said on the radio that *it was going to rain.*

2 A: I'd love to visit New Orleans.
B: I thought you said _____
_____ .

3 A: Oh, didn't you get me an ice cream?
B: But you said _____
_____ .

4 A: That's £150 for the room, including breakfast.
B: But I was told _____
_____ .

5 A: I'm afraid Mr Cooper's in a meeting.
B: But when I spoke to you earlier, you said
_____
_____ .

6 A: I can't find the letter to Sachs & Co. anywhere.
B: But you told me just now that
_____
_____ .

7 A: Let's go to the Pizza Parlour for lunch.
B: But I thought you said _____
_____ .

8 A: Come on – you'd better get a taxi or you'll miss your flight.
B: But they told me at reception _____
_____ .

I've been to New Orleans.

The room will cost £120.

It's going to rain.

The food at the Pizza Parlour is terrible.

I don't want an ice cream, thank you.

I've posted the letter to Sachs & Co.

Mr Cooper will be free at three o'clock.

You've got plenty of time to get to the airport.

5a Put the words in the right order to make reported questions.

1 me / her / She / whether / long / I'd / asked / known .
   She asked me whether I'd known her long.

2 asked / the / police officer / was / what / I / the / time .
   _____

3 witness / ever / asked / lawyer / The / the / the / man / she / seen / before / had / if .
   _____

4 often / I / asked / My / visit / grandma / don't / her / more / me / why .
   _____

5 dinner / Luc / Vanessa / asked / for / out / like / she'd / go / to / whether .
   _____

6 us / asked / challenge / thought / ready / we / whether / They / were / we / the / for .
   _____

7 Australia / The / president / Tony / asked / teacher / the / who / was / of .
   _____

8 menu / The / asked / see / whether / we'd / to / waiter / us / dessert / like / the .
   _____

b Write the actual questions the people asked.

1 *Have you known her long?*
2 _____
3 _____
4 _____
5 _____
6 _____
7 _____
8 _____

Pronunciation
Stress patterns and telling the truth

6 🎧 10.2 Listen to each sentence said twice. In which sentence does the person believe what the other person said, a or b?

1 He told her he loved her. *a*
2 Alex said he'd done his homework but had left it at home. ___
3 The government said they wouldn't raise taxes. ___
4 The witness said she'd never seen the man before. ___
5 Vanessa told her husband she had to work late that night. ___
6 Joe said he'd left his wallet at home. ___
7 They told us they'd never been here before. ___
8 Vicky told us she'd really enjoyed the meal. ___

Language focus 2
Verbs that summarise what people say

7 Six of the sentences below are wrong. Correct the mistakes, using some of the verbs in the box.

agree	assure	blame	complain	decide
deny	point out	~~promise~~	refuse	threaten
warn				

1 Simon ~~threatened~~ *promised* to bring Josie some expensive perfume from Paris.
2 The President refused having an affair with his secretary.
3 The newspaper claimed that Ms Fairchild had lied about her taxes.
4 Tony accused the late nights at his office for the breakup of his marriage.
5 Paula's friends suggested her not to go out with Jack.
6 Sonia suggested booking a table in case the restaurant got very busy.
7 The car dealer urged me that his prices were the lowest in town.
8 I'm sure we'd all like to congratulate André on winning the championship.
9 The company offered to double Jeremy's salary if he would stay on.
10 At the end of the evening, we concluded to meet the next day.

8 Complete the second sentence so that it has a similar meaning to the first, using the correct form of the summarising verbs in the box.

blame   complain   deny   offer
refuse   threaten   warn

1 Let's hire a van and travel around Europe.
He *suggested hiring a van and travelling around Europe.*

2 No, I'm not going to pay.
She _____ .

3 I didn't break the photocopier, honestly.
She _____ .

4 This food is undercooked.
She _____ .

5 Be careful Pat, the roads are very slippery.
She _____ .

6 If you don't turn that noise down, I'm going to call the police.
She _____ .

7 Would you like me to have a look at your TV?
He _____ .

8 The misunderstanding was your fault, Geoff.
She _____ .

Wordspot
speak and *talk*

9 Put a word from the box into the correct place in each sentence to make phrases with *speak* or *talk*.

about   actions   mind   ~~peace~~   point
radio   shop   show   small   terms   to
up   well

1 After six hours, there has been very little progress
peace
in the ‸talks between the two sides.
2 Is that Frank? You're on *Eastern Suburbs Talk* – what's your question for the team?
3 I've never met Stephanie, but Robert's always spoken very of her.
4 What's worrying you, Todd? Come on, you're not usually afraid to speak your.
5 Are you and Paula on speaking again yet?
6 I bought her some flowers as a way of saying sorry. After all, 'speak louder than words,' as they say.
7 Jon certainly knows what he's talking when it comes to choosing a new laptop.
8 You'll have to speak when you're giving your presentation – it's a very big room.
9 I'm sorry to talk at the weekend, but I need to ask you about the Freeman report.
10 At 9.30 we're showing ITC's new talk, hosted by comedian Dean Skinner.
11 I wasn't talking myself, I was using the earpiece on my mobile phone – look!
12 The national lottery scandal is a real talking all over the country at the moment.
13 Do we have to go to the party? You know I hate making talk with Annie and Jeff's friends.

Writing
Summarise an article

10a Read the article quickly and choose the best title.

1 Why I love ebooks. ___
2 The end of books? Perhaps not. ___
3 How television killed reading. ___

A major online bookseller recently announced that sales of ebooks are now worth more than sales of traditional paperback and hardback novels combined. So does this mean the end of the traditional paper novel as we know it?

I love the availability of ebooks, the fact that within one gadget, I can be recommended a book that I'll most likely enjoy, order it and start reading it, all in a matter of minutes. I no longer have to spend hours walking along endless shelves in a bookshop, trying to decide whether I'll actually enjoy the book I've chosen. My vocabulary has improved, too. If I come across a word I don't know, I can simply highlight it and use the built-in dictionary to get a definition. It's easier to travel light nowadays, too, as I don't have to pack any heavy books that will weigh me down – instead I just carry hundreds of books round with me in one simple gadget.

But does this really mean the book is dead? I don't think so. After all, the same thing was said about the rise of television, and radio before that. In fact, as far back as 1835, Théophile Gautier, in his novel *Mademoiselle de Maupin*, declared, 'The newspaper is killing the book, as the book killed architecture'. You see, the traditional book is a tough character. There's something almost romantic about it, whether it's the smell of its pages, or the way it's like a trusty friend that fits reassuringly under your arm on the train or bus, which tells the world a little about you by its cover. It can be an old friend that we return to when we're feeling down, and our bookshelves stand as a kind of history of our lives, with each faded cover holding memories and pleasures unique to each of us.

What the online bookseller didn't mention when reporting their sales figures is that sales of paperback and hardback books are also rising, and that this particular bookseller, while huge, has only 19% of the overall market for novels. Of course, the ebook is going to have its place in the future, but to say it will kill off the traditional novel is like saying that the invention of online poker would be the end of all casinos. Like television and radio, it will simply become another form of media we come to enjoy.

b Are these statements true (T) or false (F), according to the article?

1 The writer hates ebooks. ___
2 It only takes a few minutes to read a whole ebook. ___
3 You can carry hundreds of ebooks on one machine. ___
4 The writer only reads romance novels. ___
5 The books we keep represent things that happen in our lives. ___
6 Overall, the writer thinks that traditional paper books will always exist. ___

11a The following text is a summary of the article in Exercise 10, posted on a forum. Complete the summary with the phrases in the box.

> According to the article …   Apparently, …
> I was surprised to find that …
> I'd be interested to hear what you think.
> ~~The article is about …~~
> The main point that comes out of it is …

COMMENTS 💬

I recently read an article on the rise of ebooks which I found really interesting. ¹*This article is about* how ebooks have become very popular. ²_____ , one major online bookseller has reported that they are now selling more ebooks than traditional paperback and hardback novels.

³_____ , this has caused many people to suggest that the increase in popularity of ebooks means this might be the end of the traditional paper book. The writer disagrees with this though, and he argues that there will always be a demand for traditional books, and that people said similar things about television and radio when they appeared. In fact, ⁴_____ although more ebooks are being sold than paperback and hardback books, sales of these are also rising. ⁵_____ that although ebooks are going to become very common in the coming years, it doesn't mean that traditional novels will disappear altogether.

What do you think? Do you like ebooks or do you still prefer the reassuring feel of a paper novel? ⁶_____ .

b Think of an article you've read recently, or find one on the internet. Write a summary for a forum. Use the phrases from Exercise 11a.

Language focus 1
Hypothetical situations in the present

1a Put the words in order to make questions.

QUESTION TIME:
What if ...?

Celebrity chef Maggie Ellis answers our questions.

1 if / months / work / What / you / take / could / you / off / would / six / do / ?
   What would you do if you could take six months off work?

2 would / do / you / leader / What / a / you / world / if / became / ?
   _____

3 body / What / you / if / could / part / would / your / change / you / of / ?
   _____

4 desert / If / live / a / island, / you / with / take / on / would / what / you / had / to / you / ?
   _____

5 you / fire / from / home / on / if / What / was / it / rescue / your / would / ?
   _____

6 could / you / places / with / choose / who / If / anyone / you / change / would / ?
   _____

7 What / school / study / you / back / if / went / you / would / to / ?
   _____

8 weeks / live / if / to / only / What / you / would / had / you / four / do / ?
   _____

b Complete the answers with the correct form of the verbs in the box, then match them with the questions in part *a*.

be (x2)   can (x2)   learn   love   ~~try~~   want

a I *'d try* to make the gap between rich and poor narrower. ____

b I'd save as many of my books as I _____ . ____

c I'd eat and drink anything I _____ ! ____

d If my children _____ a bit older, I'd take them on a world tour. ____

e I think I'd take a camera, so I _____ record the experience. ____

f My hands – I _____ to have slim, elegant fingers. ____

g I _____ Italian, so I could read all those wonderful, old Italian recipe books. ____

h If it _____ just for a day, I'd choose a supermodel! ____

c 🎧 **11.1 Listen and check.**

2 Use the prompts to write complete sentences.

1 I wish / I have / curly hair.
   I wish I had curly hair.

2 If only I / can / drive.
   _____

3 I wish Sally / speak up. I can hardly hear her.
   _____

4 If only we / be / still on holiday.
   _____

5 If only I / not get / so nervous before exams.
   _____

6 I wish you / be quiet / and / listen / to me.
   _____

3 Rewrite the sentences so that they have the same meaning, using *It's time*.

1 Susan ought to get a job.
   It's time Susan got a job.

2 We'd better go home now.
   _____

3 The children should be in bed now.
   _____

4 Jo should realise that money doesn't grow on trees.
   _____

5 Why don't you learn to cook for yourself!
   _____

6 Why don't we do more to protect our environment?
   _____

Pronunciation
Vowels in science/nature words

4a Complete the chart with the words in the box, according to the <u>underlined</u> vowel sounds.

> aster<u>oi</u>d   catastroph<u>e</u>   dinos<u>au</u>r   d<u>i</u>oxide
> <s>er<u>u</u>ption</s>   f<u>ue</u>l   nucl<u>ea</u>r   oc<u>ea</u>n   r<u>a</u>dioactive
> sc<u>i</u>entific   s<u>o</u>lar   surf<u>a</u>ce   temp<u>e</u>rature
> v<u>o</u>lcanic   volcan<u>o</u>

/ɪ/ <u>e</u>xample	/ɔː/ m<u>ore</u>	/ʊə/ p<u>ure</u>	/iː/ m<u>e</u>
eruption			
/ə/ t<u>ea</u>cher	/eɪ/ s<u>ay</u>	/ɒ/ h<u>o</u>t	/ɪə/ <u>a</u>rea
/ɔɪ/ v<u>oi</u>d	/əʊ/ n<u>o</u>	/aɪ/ s<u>i</u>lent	

b 🎧 **11.2** Listen and check. Practise saying the words.

Vocabulary
Science and processes

5a Complete the descriptions with the words in the box.

> affect   <s>capture</s>   cause   combat   contribute
> disappear   impact   prevent   reflect   turn

1 These can have surfaces which *capture* sunlight and _____ it into electricity.   *d*
2 Though not yet a reality, these could be dropped from aeroplanes in order to replace forests that have _____ . The forests would then _____ CO_2 levels from getting too high.   ___
3 Burning these _____ an increase in greenhouse gases, which _____ to climate change.   ___
4 This chemical could act as a 'sunscreen' around our atmosphere to _____ sunlight. This would have a huge _____ on global temperatures.   ___
5 These tiny ocean-dwelling organisms _____ climate change by consuming CO_2 and producing oxygen, which positively _____ the level of greenhouse gases in the atmosphere.   ___

b Match the photos to the descriptions.

a) Fossil fuels

b) Titanium dioxide

c) Plankton

d) Green buildings   **e)** Tree bombs

Listen and read
Our health and well-being: facts or myths?

6a 🎧 **11.3 Listen to and/or read the extracts about health and well-being. Are these statements true (T) or false (F)?**

1 Coffee beans contain more caffeine than tea leaves. ___
2 Chocolate makes you live longer. ___
3 The best time to exercise is in the early evening. ___
4 You can get a cold from going out in the rain. ___
5 People who are allergic to pets are allergic to their fur. ___

b Listen and/or read again and answer the questions. What ...

1 should you eat three times a month?
_____

2 is 'dander'?
_____

3 might keep you awake at night?
_____

4 makes about eighty cups of coffee?
_____

5 cause colds and flu?
_____

c Answer the questions.

1 Why are we less likely to injure ourselves if we exercise at around six p.m.?
_____

2 If you are allergic to animals, is it best to have a dog or a cat as a pet?
_____

3 Can you catch a cold by shaking hands with someone?
_____

4 How are chocolate and red wine similar?
_____

5 If you want less caffeine from your tea, should you drink it immediately or make a second brew?
_____

Researchers at Harvard University, in the US, studied 8,000 men for 65 years and found those who ate modest amounts of chocolate up to three times a month lived almost a year longer than those who didn't eat any. They concluded this was likely to be because cocoa contains antioxidants called polyphenols, also found in red wine, which prevent the oxidation of harmful cholesterol.

Antioxidants are also known to protect against cancer.

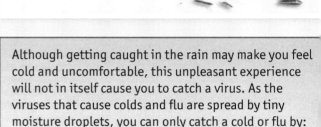

Although getting caught in the rain may make you feel cold and uncomfortable, this unpleasant experience will not in itself cause you to catch a virus. As the viruses that cause colds and flu are spread by tiny moisture droplets, you can only catch a cold or flu by:

- breathing in moisture droplets carrying the viruses (often as a result of an infected person coughing or sneezing near you) or;
- shaking hands with or touching an infected person.

More people seem to catch colds and flu in cold weather because they spend a lot of time indoors together and are therefore more likely to come into contact with viruses. Make sure you wash your hands frequently and stand back from people with coughs and sneezes.

A dog may be a man's best friend, but not if the man is among the estimated ten to fifteen percent of the population that suffers from pet allergies. The allergen is a specific protein produced not in the animal's fur, but primarily in its skin and – to a lesser extent – its saliva. As the animal is stroked or brushed, or as it rubs up against furniture or people, microscopic flakes of skin (called dander) become airborne. Since all cats and dogs have skin, there are no non-allergenic breeds.

However, since short-haired pets have less hair to shed, they send less dander into the air, so are preferable for those with pet allergies. Dogs are half as likely to cause allergic reactions as cats, but if you're allergic to furry animals, the only no-risk pets are fish and reptiles.

It depends on whether you are referring to the loose product or the brewed cup. Tea leaves have more caffeine than coffee beans before they are brewed. Prepared, however, tea is diluted quite a bit more than most coffees: a pound of tea yields 200–250 cups of tea, while a pound of coffee makes approximately eighty cups. This will of course vary depending on how strong you like your tea or coffee. It has also been found that about eighty percent of the caffeine content in tea is extracted during the first minute of brewing. So if you want to reduce your caffeine intake, one suggestion is to discard the first brew and then make another cup using the same teabag or tea leaves.

There are all kinds of popular theories: that first thing in the morning is best because you will speed up your metabolism and burn more calories all day; that exercising before dinner will reduce your appetite; that exercise in the evening won't work because it will rev you up and keep you from getting a good night's sleep. However, many experts agree that our body temperature plays an enormous part in exercise and fitness performance, and that the body performs best when its temperature is naturally higher, which is at around six p.m. Muscular temperature also affects our flexibility and strength, so we are less likely to injure ourselves at that time of day, and more likely to be able to develop a muscular physique.

Language focus 2
Hypothetical situations in the past

7 **Choose the correct ending for each sentence.**

1 If you'd told me about her situation …
   a <u>I wouldn't have said anything.</u>
   b I wouldn't said anything.

2 I wish I …
   a went to bed earlier last night. I'm really tired.
   b had gone to bed earlier last night. I'm really tired.

3 If I'd paid more attention in class …
   a I can answer this question.
   b I could answer this question.

4 I'm sure Katya would have invited you …
   a if she'd known you were in town.
   b if she knows you're in town.

5 If Ramalho hadn't missed that penalty …
   a we will have won the game.
   b we might have won the game.

6 Sitting on the beach in the rain, the Greene family …
   a wished they'd chosen another day to come.
   b wish they would choose another day to come.

7 We would have tried to get here sooner …
   a if we'd known you were waiting.
   b if we've known you were waiting.

8 If you hadn't been using your mobile while driving …
   a you would see the motorbike pull out in front.
   b you would have seen the motorbike pull out in front.

8 Complete the sentences with the correct form of the verbs in the box.

ask   be   ~~call~~   get   go   know   listen
look   mention   miss   notice   offer
tell (x2)   wake

1 Thank you for your help last night: if you *hadn't* *called* _____ the police so quickly, there might _____ a fight.

2 I wish you _____ me about the surprise party for Marta – I'm no good at keeping secrets!

3 A: Please don't wake me up too early tomorrow, Mum.
  B: Look, if I _____ you at six this morning, you would _____ the train!

4 Why did you tell Josef about the scratch on the car? If you _____ it, he _____ anything!

5 A: I wish I _____ my boss that I can speak Korean.
  B: Why not?
  A: Well, then he wouldn't _____ me to translate all these boring documents.
  B: But he wouldn't _____ to send you on a marketing trip to Seoul, either!

6 If only Nathan _____ to my advice – I'm sure he would _____ the job.

7 A: If you _____ about the storm, _____ you _____ sailing?
  B: No! I wish I _____ at the weather forecast.

9 In these hypothetical situations, complete the two possible endings (one present and one past) with the correct form of the verbs in brackets.

1 If Julie and Sam hadn't had that terrible row,
  a they *wouldn't have split up* .
  b they _____ together now. (not split up / still be)

2 If the banks had been more honest,
  a we _____ in such a mess.
  b the stock market _____ . (not be / not collapse)

3 If Ed had given up smoking ten years ago,
  a he _____ such bad asthma now.
  b he _____ hundreds of pounds. (not have / save)

4 If I'd worked harder at school,
  a I _____ my exams.
  b I _____ a better job. (pass / have)

5 If Tammi had made a back-up copy of her files,
  a she _____ them all.
  b she _____ them now. (not lose / not retype)

Wordspot
life

10 Choose the correct alternative to complete the sentences.

1 TV chefs make cooking look easy on their TV programmes, but in **your private life / real life** it's never that easy.

2 The **lifeguard / life jacket** blew his whistle and told the children to stop fighting in the pool.

3 Don't worry, you've got an infection, but it's nothing **life-threatening / life-like**.

4 Be nice to her. She's the accommodation officer and can make **a life sentence / life difficult** for you if she wants to.

5 Helena was thrilled when they offered her a part in the movie. **It was the chance of a lifetime! / That's life!**

6 Have you seen this painting? It's so **real life / life-like** I thought it was a photo!

7 I don't believe in the death penalty. I think a **life expectancy / life sentence** is a much more effective deterrent.

8 At the age of 76, my grandfather finally fulfilled his **lifelong / life-like** ambition of doing a parachute jump.

Language live
Reporting opinions

11a Read the results of a survey about celebrities.

Statement	Agree	Disagree	Don't know/ depends
It's easy to become famous these days.	20%	40%	10%
We attach too much importance to celebrities nowadays.	54%	40%	6%
Celebrities should be allowed to keep their privacy.	28%	68%	4%
Too many people are famous for the wrong reasons.	25%	75%	0%
A politician is more important to society than an actor.	60%	30%	10%
Rich celebrities should be made to donate some of their income to charity.	85%	10%	5%

b Complete the information from the table using the phrases in the box.

....

One in five   A quarter   Just over half
On the whole   The vast majority   Three out of five

....

1 *One in five* people think it's easy to become famous these days.
2 _____ the people polled said we attach too much importance to celebrities nowadays.
3 _____ people don't agree that celebrities should be allowed to keep their privacy.
4 _____ of people think that too many people are famous for the wrong reasons.
5 _____ people think a politician is more important to society than an actor.
6 _____ of people think rich celebrities should be made to donate some of their income to charity.

Writing
A for and against essay

12a Read the essay below and match the purposes in the checklist with each paragraph.

1 arguments against the statement ____
2 introduction to the topic of the essay ____
3 conclusion, in which the writer introduces his/her opinion ____
4 arguments in favour of the statement ____

TOO YOUNG TO CHANGE?

A In today's society, image is more important than ever before. With a growing online presence for most young people comes the importance of 'looking good', and as a consequence of this, many young people turn to cosmetic surgery in order to maintain the 'perfect' image. This essay will explore the arguments for and against the statement: People should be allowed to have cosmetic surgery before the age of eighteen.

B There are several arguments in favour of the statement. ^{1} First of all, if a child was disfigured in some way, and was being bullied at school, then cosmetic surgery would be justified. ^{2} _____ , surgery may sometimes be necessary for medical reasons. ^{3} _____ , a person might not be able to breathe because of the shape of their nose. ^{4} _____ , if someone is old enough to drive or get married at sixteen, then they should be able to decide for themselves about cosmetic surgery.

C ^{5} _____ , it's important to ^{6} _____ , that an impressionable teenager may make a decision because of peer pressure, then regret it later in life. ^{7} _____ , young people would not be able to cope with the risks and possible side effects connected with cosmetic surgery. ^{8} _____ , society should not encourage young people to see appearance as more important than anything else.

D ^{9} _____ , there are strong arguments on both sides of the debate, but ^{10} _____ , the arguments against cosmetic surgery under the age of eighteen are more serious than those for, and so it should not be allowed.

b How many arguments were given in favour of the statement, and how many were given against it?

In favour: ____
Against: ____

c Complete the gaps in the essay with a word/phrase in the box.

....

Also   Another argument is that   First of all
However   For example   Furthermore   Secondly
In conclusion   in my opinion   remember

....

Vocabulary

Fame

1a Match the beginnings in A with the endings in B to make phrases related to fame.

A

1 be in the media _d_
2 draw huge ____
3 have a reputation ____
4 an overnight ____
5 be ill-equipped to deal ____
6 act like a ____
7 make a ____
8 a household ____
9 be splashed across the ____

B

a sensation   **f** for doing something
b crowds   **g** newspapers
c name   **h** diva
d spotlight   **i** with something
e comeback

b Complete the newspaper article below with phrases from exercise 1a in the correct form.

Soul legend found dead in LA hotel room

Victoria Gold, the multiple platinum-selling musician, was found dead this morning in her hotel suite in Los Angeles. Gold, a [1]_household name_ in soul music, whose concerts continued to [2]_____ well into the 2000s, had just started a world tour to coincide with the release of her new album, Proud. The cause of death is not known, but at the age of 70, it is believed she died of natural causes.

Gold became an [3]_____ in 1976 when the release of her debut single You've gotta love me shot her to fame in the US. In the following years, she went through a very public divorce and often found herself [4]_____ across the _____ with stories of bad behaviour, which made many people think

she was [5]_____ to _____ the pressures of fame.

However, despite having a [6]_____ for acting like a [7]_____ she went on to prove her critics wrong, and her 1981 album Gifted is considered to be the seminal soul album of the era.

The end of the 1990s and the new millennium saw her [8]_____ a _____ with the release of a new album and subsequent tour with the band The Late Nights attracting a new generation of fans. Victoria Gold was once again in the [9]_____ .

Victoria Gold is survived by her three daughters and seven grandchildren.

Listen and read

5 steps to making a viral video

2a 🎧 12.1 Listen to and/or read the web article. Put the five steps in the correct places 1–5 in the text.

- Emphasise the spark
- Know your audience
- Check for copycats
- Choose the right spark
- Create a meme

b Listen and/or read again. Are these statements true (T) or false (F), according to the article?

1 The writer doesn't think it's likely that you've ever created a popular video clip. ____
2 You only need to think about who will watch your video if you don't want it to be popular. ____
3 Everybody loves cute videos. ____
4 It's good if your video makes the viewer react physically. ____
5 The volume settings should be loud. ____
6 It's good if lots of people copy your idea. ____

c Match phrases 1–5 from the article in *a* with the definitions a–e.

1 chances are, ...
2 hit a nerve
3 have limited/universal appeal
4 create a buzz
5 soundtrack
a liked by only a certain type of person/liked by everybody
b the music to accompany a video
c It's likely
d generate a lot of discussion about something
e mention a subject which people feel strongly about

5 STEPS TO MAKING A VIRAL VIDEO

Have you ever uploaded a funny or interesting video clip to a video sharing website? Chances are that if you did, it got viewed by some of your friends who you showed it to, but not many people picked up on it from outside your social circle. So what is it that makes some videos go viral? Why do some videos get viewed several million times, especially when they look like they've been put together by a bored teenager at home, with nothing better to do? I spoke to Danika Holmes, a social media analyst with a special interest in video, to ask her advice on what to do if I wanted to make a viral video. Here's what she said.

1 _____

Think about who will be watching your video so you know who to aim it at. Even if you're going for universal appeal, you need to start with a specific, targeted viewer base. Think about what makes these types of people tick and what they like to talk about with their friends.

2 _____

Once you've got to know your audience, you'll need to choose the right entertainment aspect to hit a nerve – the right spark. The four most common sparks are funny, sexy, surprising and random. Cute often makes an appearance as well, but this can have limited appeal to some audiences.

3 _____

Once you've chosen the spark, you need to focus on this aspect and emphasise it. There's no point in your video being 'quite' funny – it's all or nothing. As a general rule, your video should be able to cause a physical reaction such as laughter, crying, a shocked expression, etc.

4 _____

A meme is an iconic symbol of a culture at a specific time, which gets passed on from person to person. This is exactly what you want to happen to your video, so create a buzz, and turn up the volume. Share comments on it on microblogging and social networking websites and encourage other people to do the same.

5 _____

This is the true test of whether your video has gone viral. If people copy your video, wearing different clothes, or acting it out in different situations, or remix to a different soundtrack, then you know you've created a viral video. At the height of the Harlem Shake meme in early 2013, 4,000 copies were being uploaded a day around the world. This also ensures your viral video will be remembered in years to come. And in today's fast-paced, throw-away society, that's quite an achievement.

Language focus 1
Use of gerunds and infinitives

3 Complete the gaps with the verbs in the box, with or without *to*.

answer   be   believe   borrow   come
eat   find   go   ~~land~~   offer   read
see   suggest   tell   thank   think

1 The President's plane is expected *to land* at 9:30 tonight.
2 Thank you for the advice about Jess. Your comments really made me _____ .
3 I passed Maria in the street today, but she pretended _____ me.
4 I thought it was a very difficult exam. How many questions did you manage _____ ?
5 I think I'll buy Tessa some flowers _____ her for helping with Kim's party.
6 I told Vikki what Kate said about the redundancies at work, but she refused _____ me.
7 I'll let you _____ the car as long as you promise _____ careful with it.
8 Is it really necessary _____ every page of the document? It'll take ages!
9 Are you hungry? Can I get you something _____ ?
10 I understand your problem, but I really don't know what _____ .
11 Roy's Café is fine, but wouldn't you rather _____ somewhere special for your birthday?
12 I've had a row with Todd's brother and now he's threatening _____ to our wedding.
13 Why don't you use the internet _____ the information you need for your project?
14 It's not easy for me _____ you this, but we've decided _____ you the job.

4 Choose the correct alternative.

The Prime Minister was asked today how he plans ¹*deal with* / (*to deal with*) / *dealing with* growing crime amongst teenagers. He believes that it is important ²*create* / *to create* / *creating* more jobs and ³*provide* / *to provide* / *providing* more opportunities for them ⁴*get* / *to get* / *getting* work. At the same time he thinks that we should ⁵*be sent* / *to be sent* / *be sending* young criminals to prison for longer. 'This government is tough on crime', is his slogan. Parents must continue ⁶*play* / *to play* / *playing* a vital role in ⁷*help* / *to help* / *helping* the government ⁸*make* / *to make* / *making* our streets safer. The government is also considering ⁹*introduce* / *to introduce* / *introducing* a curfew in some city centres ¹⁰*stop* / *to stop* / *stopping* young people being out on the streets after 11 o'clock, when most serious crimes happen.

5 Rewrite the sentences so that the meaning stays the same, using the word in bold.

1 I read this article and I didn't look up any words in my dictionary. **without**
   I read this article without looking up any words in my dictionary.

2 In the summer you shouldn't go out in the midday sun. **avoid**
   In the _____ .

3 Al said he didn't eat the rest of the chocolates. **deny**
   _____ .

4 I'm finding it less strange to drive an automatic car. **getting used**
   I'm _____ .

5 I lost weight because I did lots of exercise and counted calories. **by**
   I lost _____ .

6 Tickets sell out quickly, so it's useful to phone the box office to check first. **worth**
   Tickets sell out _____ .

7 I'm sorry, madam, it's difficult for me to find your details on the computer. **trouble**
   I'm sorry, madam, _____ .

8 If it's not a problem for you to wait, I can get you a table next to the window. **don't mind**
   If _____ .

9 Do you think that you might apply for the job in Madrid? **considering**
   Are _____ ?

10 One of the best things about the summer is that you can eat outside. **able**
   One of the best things _____ .

11 You're going to see all your old school friends tomorrow. Are you excited? **looking forward**
   Are you _____ ?

12 I feel sad because I don't have the beach opposite my apartment any more. **miss**
   I _____ .

6 Complete the gaps with the verbs in the box in the infinitive (with or without *to*) or gerund form.

~~find~~   cheat   find out   get   leave (x2)
meet (x2)   play   spend   trust   try

it's only a gameshow

BIG BROTHER
ruined my love life, says Nasty Nick

Big Brother celebrity Nick Bateman says it's now impossible for him ¹*to find* a girlfriend because of his image. Bateman, a contestant on the reality show in which ten people agree ²_____ twelve weeks together in a house full of cameras, was dubbed 'Nasty Nick' after he was made ³_____ the house for ⁴_____ to influence the other contestants' eviction nominations. Since ⁵_____ the house, Bateman has earned good money by ⁶_____ on his evil image but his reputation has made it difficult for women ⁷_____ him. 'Before BB, I had no trouble ⁸_____ women, but now they can't ⁹_____ away fast enough,' he told The People magazine. 'It would be great ¹⁰_____ a woman who can see beyond what happened all those years ago and take time ¹¹_____ who I really am.' Bateman, who still receives hate mail, added, '¹²_____ is wrong and I'm sorry I did it, but I thought I was just playing the game.'

Language focus 2
Different infinitive and gerund forms

7a Find the mistakes in six of these sentences and correct them.

1 It's important not ~~to~~ ^y focus too much on the negative aspects. Think about the positives, too.

2 I've often wondered what it would be like to lock up in a house for twelve weeks with nine strangers.

3 One thing I love about weekends is not waking up by an alarm clock.

4 Despite having done a lot of charity work in his life, he is best remembered for his music.

5 Marsha says she likes not to be responsible for other people in her new job, but I don't really believe her.

6 I expected you to have finished that hours ago: why is it taking so long?

7 I don't want to worry you, but there's a huge, black rain cloud over there and it seems to come towards us.

8 I'd like to learn more about ancient Greek philosophy when I was at university.

b 🎧 **12.2 Listen and check.**

8a Complete the sentences with the correct form of the verb in brackets.

1 In France, it is always worth _carrying_ (carry) a few euros for tips to taxi drivers, and it is customary _____ (give) a couple of euros to the cinema usher who shows you to your seat.

2 In the United States, it is not uncommon to see people _____ (chase) out of a restaurant by waiters for failing _____ (leave) a tip.

3 Life gets tricky in Japan, where people are expected _____ (show) gratitude, rather than actually hand over money.

4 How much _____ (tip) and when have always been tricky questions for the British.

5 Attitudes to tipping seem _____ (change) a lot in the UK over the last twenty years.

6 And finally, what are visitors to the UK advised _____ (do)?

7 Should tips _____ (include) in the minimum wage?

8 Holidays in the Middle East, where tipping is expected by nearly everyone, can _____ (get) very expensive.

9 Travellers to Scandinavia, where the cost of living is high, may _____ (be) relieved to find that tipping is not expected.

10 The report also angered waiters, waitresses and hairdressers by _____ (suggest) that tips should _____ (include) in the minimum hourly rate.

b The sentences in part *a* have been removed from the article on the right about tipping. Decide where the sentences go in the text. There is one sentence which you do not need to use.

Some handy tips about tipping

The low pay debate highlights the practice that varies widely

a _7_
This was the question being fiercely debated when the Government and unions clashed over the Low Pay Commission's report this week. The report suggests a minimum wage of £6.19 an hour, disappointing unions, which are campaigning for £7.10.

b ___
This will particularly affect those who work in restaurants where a service charge is included in the bill.

c ___
These issues are all the more topical because millions of them will soon be setting off on summer holidays to countries where customs vary widely. Here are some general guidelines on what to do.

d ___
The advice I was given by an American friend was: 'If in doubt, leave a tip.' This is a general rule of thumb. At a bar, for example, staff will expect you to leave them the change.

e ___
However, French law requires that restaurants, cafés and hotel bills include the service charge, usually 10–15 percent, so a tip is not expected.

f ___
For the more penny-pinching traveller, try Yemen, the only country in the region without a strong tipping culture.

g ___
There can be a serious loss of face for the people involved, such as waiters, if you try to insist on giving them a tip.

h ___
Hairdressers and people who work in restaurants will probably think you are mad if you try to leave a tip.

i ___
The popular travel guide *The Lonely Planet* has these suggestions. You should tip 10–15 percent of the total bill in a restaurant and round up taxi fares to the nearest 50p.

Pronunciation

Sentence stress

9a Underline the stressed words in the sentences below.

1 She <u>agreed</u> to be <u>interviewed</u>.
2 You should focus on winning the race.
3 We'd like to have known about it sooner.
4 I hate being told what to do.
5 You promised not to be late.
6 I want to be lying on a beach right now.

b 🎧 **12.3 Listen and check. Practise saying the sentences with the correct stress.**

Writing

A forum post

10a Look at the list of discussion topics on the forum below. Which of the questions do the forum posts answer?

The People's Forum

Discussion topic: FAME

- Does becoming famous depend on luck or hard work?
- What would you like to be famous for?
- Why is being famous so important to some people?
- Will the internet ever be more important in creating celebrities than TV?
- Do celebrities have the right to a private life?

A

COMMENTS 📝
....

BOOTSYJAM
17:45

I don't think I ¹**will / would** enjoy being famous at all, I hate being the centre of attention so I would hate being in the media spotlight.

However, if I was going to be famous for something, then it would have to be for making a positive difference to the world around me. To my ²**mind / brain** it would be best to be remembered for changing people's lives for the better, whether it's raising money for charity, or changing the way people think about something, I'm not sure how. It just ³**appears / seems** wrong to me to be famous for doing something not very important, like being fashionable and singing a song.

B

COMMENTS 📝
....

SHODFATHER
22:20

I don't like ⁴**a / the** way that some people say that if you're famous, you don't deserve to keep your privacy, and you shouldn't be surprised when a photo of you going shopping is splashed across the newspapers. I imagine it's very ⁵**stressed / stressful** being a celebrity. OK, so they earn a lot of money, but it can't be very easy to be recognised wherever you go. Personally, I would find to ⁶**be / being** followed by photographers all the time very difficult.

I think we need to remember that celebrities are human beings too, and there are times in their lives when they also need privacy.

b Underline the correct alternatives to complete the forum posts.

c Choose two of the discussion questions in 10a and write a forum post in reply to each.

COMMENTS 📝
....

COMMENTS 📝
....

Audio script

UNIT 1 RECORDING 1

I = Interviewer **C** = Celine **R** = Robert

I: Have you ever been on a first date with someone you really liked and found that it turned into a disaster before your very eyes? We interviewed two people who have had just this experience.

C: The worst first date I've ever had was while I was on holiday in Majorca. I must have been about eighteen, and I met this gorgeous Spanish waiter, Rodrigo. He was a good ten years older than me and had dark brown eyes and black curly hair. Well, after we'd had a few drinks in a local bar, he suggested going for a romantic walk along the beach. Things seemed to be going quite well, even though we didn't have much in common. Then we walked past a couple of guys who were standing at the water's edge talking. When they looked across at us, Rodrigo stared at them aggressively. He asked them what their problem was, and what they were looking at. They hadn't even been looking at us before that, but he started arguing with them. His behaviour was a real turn-off and made me uncomfortable. I felt so ashamed that I just walked away. I never dated Rodrigo again, as you can imagine.

R: She was someone I knew from school and I'd always really fancied her. I had just got a new motorbike, a Suzuki 250, which I was really proud of. So anyway, one Saturday afternoon, I asked her to come out for a ride and we went up to a disused airfield a few kilometres away. There was no one else around, so I started driving with one wheel in the air and going really fast. Claire said she loved it and could she have a go at riding it. I couldn't see why not – but how wrong can you be? Once she'd managed to start it and stay upright, she suddenly got a bit over-confident and zoomed off at top speed towards some trees. As I started running after her, I could see that she was losing control of the bike, and a minute later – bang! She went straight into a tree. Claire was a bit shocked and bruised, but my beautiful Suzuki was a wreck and cost me a fortune to repair. We did see each other again, but from then on we stuck to public transport.

UNIT 1 RECORDING 2

1 **A:** How do you feel today?
   B: Much better, thanks.
2 **A:** Do you love me?
   B: Of course I do.
3 **A:** I don't believe it! Chelsea are losing!
   B: Are they? I thought they'd win this easily!
4 **A:** She doesn't like me, does she?
   B: Yes she does, don't be silly.
5 **A:** Trudi's not a very good singer.
   B: Yes she is! How can you say that?
6 **A:** You're not listening to me, love.
   B: I am listening to you!

UNIT 1 RECORDING 3

1 **A:** I'm sorry! I've spilt my coffee all over your tablecloth.
   B: Never mind. It's easily washable.
2 **A:** I can't stop thinking about Helen's operation.
   B: Try not to worry about it. There's nothing you can do.
3 **A:** The kids at school keep laughing at my hair.
   B: Oh, don't take any notice of them.
4 **A:** I think my boss heard me saying that he annoys me.
   B: He probably didn't hear you. There's no point in getting upset about it.
5 **A:** I've got to have four teeth out tomorrow.
   B: That sounds awful!
6 **A:** My son is going into hospital for tests next week.
   B: You must be really worried.
7 **A:** I can't believe we're not going to have you as our teacher any more.
   B: Cheer up! Your new teacher's really nice.
8 **A:** I just can't do it! I'm too nervous! Someone else will have to give the speech.
   B: Calm down! You'll be fine.
9 **A:** Andy said my dress makes me look fat!
   B: Just ignore him. You look perfect!
10 **A:** Our car won't be ready until the weekend.
   B: How annoying!
11 **A:** I'm so sorry. I completely forgot to bring that book you wanted to borrow.
   B: Don't worry, it doesn't matter.
12 **A:** The date was going really well, until he started telling me about his political views.
   B: What a shame! I guess you won't be seeing him again, then.

UNIT 2 RECORDING 1

hopeful	hopeless
secure	insecure
efficient	inefficient
successful	unsuccessful
solved	unsolved
enthusiastic	unenthusiastic
comfortable	uncomfortable
patient	impatient
honest	dishonest

UNIT 2 RECORDING 2

P = Pete **M** = Mel **L** = Lisa **S** = Steve **Sa** = Sandy **A** = Anna

A

P: In *It's a Wonderful Life* with James Stewart, the scene that gets me is at the end when one guy says: 'To my big brother, George, the richest man in town.' It kills me, man. In the film, it's Christmas and James Stewart is in big trouble financially and he's going to be arrested and so he decides to kill himself. But then this angel comes down (only he looks like an ordinary guy) and shows him what life would have been like in his home town if he'd never lived. And he sees how his life has touched all these other lives and really made a difference. I watch most of the film with a lump in my throat. Brilliant!

B

M: One of the funniest moments, I think, is in the first *Indiana Jones* movie, *Raiders of the Lost Ark*, when Harrison Ford is trying to escape from his enemies. It takes place in an eastern market and Indiana is suddenly faced by an enormous man wearing a turban and carrying a huge sword. The man gives an awesome display of swordplay with this sword and you can see this feeling of panic passing over Indiana's face. Then he suddenly pulls out a gun and just shoots the guy. The first time I saw it, the audience broke out in a cheer. Amazing! Apparently, I read later, they were going to do a full fight, but Ford didn't want to spend hours in the scorching sun and it would have been very expensive, so he asked Spielberg (the director) if he could just shoot the guy and Spielberg agreed.

C

L: The opening of *Jaws*. It's all in the music, which is played on the cello. I expect everyone knows it. You start by seeing the sea from the point of view of a shark on the bottom of the sea bed. Then the scene moves to a beach and it's a sunny day and all these families are sunbathing and having a good time. Then there's a girl who goes into the water, and suddenly we're under the water again, looking at the girl's legs from the shark's point of view. Then suddenly she screams and she's dragged across the surface of the water before she disappears. I was on the edge of my seat. It's much more effective than showing the shark straightaway. And for the rest of the film, every time that music comes back you know something awful is going to happen.

D

S: *Star Wars*, every time. Not the later films, but the very first film right at the end when Luke Skywalker joins the rebel attack on the Death Star. The Death Star is this huge artificial 'moon' which is about to destroy the rebels' planet. And the only way to destroy it is for the X-wing pilots to fly down a narrow lane and hit a tiny opening. All of Luke's fellow-pilots are killed or their X-wings are damaged and it's up to him alone. He makes the decision to switch off his computer and use 'the Force' to find his target. 'Great shot, kid!' says Han Solo. 'That was one in a million!'

E

Sa: The most I've ever cried in a movie was in *Pay it Forward*. It's about this kid, Trevor, and on his first day of school he gets this assignment: 'Think of an idea to change the world, and put it into practice.' And he has this idea that the world would change if everyone did good deeds for three other people, and then those three people would help three other people, and so on, and eventually it would spread right round the world. And then he gets killed trying to help a friend. And they ask everyone who has received an act of kindness or help as a result of his idea to light a candle and you see all these thousands of candles. I tell you, no one had a dry eye in the cinema.

F

A: *Jurassic Park*. The bit when the two kids are in the jeep and it's broken down and there's some water in the back and you hear this thumping noise, and all you see is the movement in the water and the fear in their eyes when they understand what it means. I saw it when I was about 11 and I was petrified. That was more frightening than actually seeing the Tyrannosaurus rex.

UNIT 2 RECORDING 3

anxiety, reality, relationship, economist
pessimism, criticism
aggression, contentment, conformist
loneliness, violence

UNIT 3 RECORDING 1

1   **Family accidentally sold teddy bear containing $50,000 in cash**

An Alaskan family accidentally sold an old teddy bear containing $50,000 in cash at a church jumble sale. Wan Song had borrowed the money for her husband's cancer treatment and had hidden it inside the bear. But she hadn't told her husband, Inhong Song, who gave the bear to the church sale in their home town of Anchorage.

Mrs Song is now appealing for whoever bought the bear to return it to the family. She had borrowed the money from friends and relatives without her husband's knowledge, to pay for surgery he needed for cancer of the pancreas.

For safekeeping, she wrapped the money in foil and sewed it inside one of their children's old teddy bears which she then hid at the back of a cupboard. Meanwhile, the family decided to help their local church jumble sale and Mrs Song packed up some items, which her husband delivered.

But when the jumble sale began to run out of items, he went back to the house, found the bear and brought it to the sale.

An older woman with two girls reportedly bought it for a dollar.

2   **Lottery syndicate robbed of winnings at celebration party**

An Italian lottery syndicate won and then lost a fortune when members were robbed at gunpoint as they divided up their $60,000 winnings. Five masked gunmen burst into the celebration party at a social club as the money was being handed out in envelopes, and grabbed the cash before escaping in a waiting car.

Syndicate organiser Vincenzo Paviglianiti said: 'We were just about to start handing out the money when five men burst in wearing masks. At first everyone laughed because they thought it was part of the party, but then the men started shouting and telling everyone to get on the floor and not to move. It was only after one of them fired a shot into the air that everyone realised it wasn't a joke. They took all the money, but at least no one was hurt.'

Police said the forty-strong syndicate may have been the victim of its own generosity after advertising the party on posters at Reggio Calabria in southern Italy. A spokesman said: 'The syndicate had put up posters and balloons in the streets around their local social club and had invited neighbours to come and celebrate their win with them. In effect, the robbers knew what was going to happen and that the money was going to be divided up at the celebration.'

3   **Man loses $10,000 engagement ring in taxi**

A man who'd saved up for over a year to buy a $10,000 engagement ring for his girlfriend lost it in a taxi in Chicago. Eric Culbertson put the ring – a platinum band with a round-cut diamond – into his wallet as he got into the taxi. He was taking girlfriend Krista Saputo to a restaurant where he'd intended to propose. But after leaving the taxi, he realised the ring was no longer in his wallet.

The twenty-eight-year-old had paid for a suite at a city hotel and arranged for chocolate-covered strawberries and champagne for their arrival. He'd also booked a table at a restaurant in the city, says the *Chicago Tribune*.

The following day, the couple travelled to Pleasant Prairie, Wisconsin for a family reunion. There, Culbertson bought a twenty-five-dollar cubic zirconia ring and asked Saputo to marry him. She accepted.

UNIT 3 RECORDING 2

1   **A:** I'm sorry sir, but there's no reservation under that name.
    B: What do you mean? My company made the reservation last week over the phone.
    A: Well, I'm sorry, but we have no record of that.
    B: Well, it's not my fault that you haven't recorded it properly. Do you have no available rooms?
    A: Well, let me see what I can do.
2   **A:** What's this? A parking ticket?
    B: Yes, sir. You've overstayed the 45 minutes that you paid for.
    A: I understand that, but I'm only two minutes late!
    B: Sorry sir, but you cannot park for longer than the time you pay for.
    A: Can I make a suggestion? Why don't I pay for another 45 minutes now, and then everyone's happy.
    B: OK, just this once, then.
3   **A:** That'll be £175, please.
    B: What? But you haven't repaired the washing machine. I don't think that's fair.
    A: I realise that, but we charge £175 for a call-out at the weekend.
    B: But this is ridiculous! I work during the week, and I'm only here at the weekend!
    A: Look, I'll tell you what. Let me repair it then we can discount this charge from the repair bill.

UNIT 3 RECORDING 3

1   a   *[angrily]* What do you mean?
    b   *[calmly]* What do you mean?
2   a   *[calmly]* Well, it's not my fault …
    b   *[angrily]* Well, it's not my fault …
3   a   *[calmly]* I understand that …
    b   *[angrily]* I understand that …
4   a   *[angrily]* Can I make a suggestion?
    b   *[calmly]* Can I make a suggestion?
5   a   *[calmly]* I don't think that's fair.
    b   *[angrily]* I don't think that's fair.
6   a   *[angrily]* But this is ridiculous.
    b   *[calmly]* But this is ridiculous.

UNIT 4 RECORDING 1

1   Several famous pictures of water lilies were painted by Monet.
2   Portuguese is spoken in Brazil.
3   The structure of DNA has been known about for more than sixty years.
4   At the moment, more tablets are being bought than ever before.
5   New Zealand was originally inhabited by Maoris.
6   The 2022 World Cup won't be held in Brazil.
7   Humans had already arrived in the Americas before Christopher Columbus 'discovered' them in 1492.
8   The part of James Bond in the 2012 film, *Skyfall* was played by Daniel Craig.

Audio script

UNIT 4 RECORDING 2

Driving Each Other Crazy

There's a well-known joke: A woman is driving down a motorway and her husband phones her on her mobile. 'Darling, be careful!' he screams, 'I've just heard there's a car driving the wrong way on the motorway near where you are.' 'It's not just one car,' she says, 'there are hundreds of them!'

And here's another one: a man is driving his daughter and they are stuck in traffic. The little girl says, 'I have a question.' 'What is it?' asks her father. 'When you're driving, are YOU ever the stupid idiot?'

Why do we laugh at these jokes? Is it because we recognise some truth in them? A lot of people seem to think that men and women do display quite different characteristics when it comes to driving, and in general, both male and female drivers tend to be quite critical of the opposite sex.

'Men are too confident in their own abilities. They never listen, they never need a map. They're always sure they know the way,' says Cathy, whose husband rarely lets her drive the car. 'They tend to drive too close to the car in front and they're incredibly impatient. If there's a car in front, they have to pass it even if it doesn't make a difference to their overall speed. I think it's some sort of territorial thing – you know, they have to be king of the road and everybody else on the road is an idiot.'

Danielle, a businesswoman who drives a BMW, agrees: 'Men never indicate before they turn left and they tend to brake at the very last minute. If I'm in a car with a man, I often feel quite nervous. I'd much rather be driven by a woman.'

It seems as if insurance companies would agree. Apparently, whilst the number of accidents men and women have tend to be about equal, the accidents which involve women are generally relatively minor and they are therefore less expensive to insure. In contrast, men tend to have more serious accidents and the worst offenders are young men, aged between 18 and 25.

What do men think about women? Interestingly, one of their main concerns is about women as passengers. 'Women passengers can't keep quiet,' says Paul, a retired architect. 'You know: "You're going too fast"' "Can you see that pedestrian?", "Didn't you see that traffic light?" or "I feel sick. Can't you go straight?" There's always some comment.'

Pete agrees: 'And women are hopeless with directions. I think it's because they're nervous about going to new places. I reckon men are better at finding new places and women are better at finding places they've been to before.'

Certainly it seems to be the case that if a man fails to follow directions, it's because his female passenger did not convey them properly. But what about women's driving? Pete again: 'My girlfriend has some strange habits, like switching on the windscreen wipers as a signal that she intends to turn right. Then she gets annoyed when she's driving and I 'brake' – you know, put my foot down as if I'm braking – when she's going round corners. I mean, one of us has to!'

Despite men's generally high opinion of their own driving skills, a report published in 2004 came down firmly in favour of women drivers. According to the report, women score more highly than men on almost all counts. These included driving within the speed limits, overtaking safely, and conducting different manoeuvres successfully, including signalling in good time, reversing and braking quickly. They also had a better awareness of other drivers on the road. There was only one aspect of driving where women did not perform as successfully as men and that was – no surprise here – the ability to park their cars. When it comes to driving, it seems that men and women may indeed come from different planets!

UNIT 4 RECORDING 3

1 A: You look different. Have you had your hair cut?
    B: Yes. What do you think?
2 A: You look pleased with yourself.
    B: Yes, I've finally got an article published in the local newspaper!
3 A: Can you have these business cards printed for me?
    B: Yes, when do you want them done by?
4 A: Oh no! I'm so sorry – all over your shirt!
    B: It really doesn't matter.
    A: No, I'll pay for you to get it cleaned.

5 A: I'm sorry about the noise.
    B: Yes, what's going on?
    A: We're having some shelves put up.
6 A: I'm not sure about this contract they want me to sign.
    B: Me neither. I'd have it checked by a lawyer, if I were you.

UNIT 4 RECORDING 4

rebellious, resilient
uncommunicative
creativity, argumentative
logic, needy, spatial
extrovert, humorous, talkative
absent-minded, open-minded, self-sufficient

UNIT 5 RECORDING 1

The weird ways people meet

People always regret asking me and my wife how we got together. It's a long story, involving other relationships and several countries, and to be honest, it's not that interesting, so I'll spare you the details. We were at a restaurant in Tuscany on our summer holiday last year though, when we met another English couple who had a far more interesting story than us. Lynn and Andy had actually met online before they got together, or at least they thought they had. After a few casual conversations through an online dating agency, they decided to meet for real. Lynn arrived at the restaurant first, and shortly after was approached by Andy, who thought she was someone else. It turns out they'd both arranged to meet different people, but liked the look of each other, and that was that!

And they're not alone. It seems there are all sorts of places you might meet that special someone. Lukas met Sofie for the first time when he crashed into her car – on his bicycle. 'It was raining and I was coming downhill really fast, so I couldn't really see where I was going. Sofie opened her car door and I went straight into it, and off my bike.' explains Lukas, 'I was unconscious for a few seconds, and when I came round there was this beautiful young woman asking me 'Are you OK?' Well, after that, she went to the hospital with me and was just really kind, really caring, and we hit it off.'

Every cloud has a silver lining, so they say, and Nick McKiddie would most likely agree. He was leaving the office late one night when he got robbed by a group of young men. He wasn't hurt, but they stole his phone and wallet, so he called the police. Susan Harris, a young police officer at the time, attended the call. Nick explains, 'I don't know whether I was in shock because of what had happened, but I think it was love at first sight. I would never usually be so confident, but I just asked if she wanted to go for a drink sometime, and to my surprise, she said yes!' Nick and Susan got married last December.

It seems crime can indeed bring people together. I know a couple who started dating after doing jury service on a particularly lengthy court case. They were spending so much time together during the trial, that when it finally ended, they realised they were really missing each other!

Animals don't have the same social inhibitions as humans do, and this was certainly the case when Ri took her dog, Ben, to the local dog park. 'As soon as I took his lead off, he ran straight to another dog on the other side of the park, and started getting very friendly indeed' she laughs, 'I actually had to pull him away, and that was when I met Ben, the other dog's owner. We had a good laugh about it all, especially when we realised he had the same name as my dog. We became friends after that, and well, the rest is history.'

UNIT 5 RECORDING 2

1 He said it was just a little white lie?
2 She's doing your head in?
3 They're hopelessly in love with each other?
4 His jokes didn't make me laugh.
5 She doesn't cry very often.
6 She hasn't had plastic surgery?
7 He's feeling really stressed out.
8 He spent the whole time dreaming about someone else?

UNIT 5 RECORDING 3

a **A:** I'm sorry, Mr Grady is busy at the moment. Could you call back a bit later on?

   B: When would be a good time to call?

b **A:** Hello, Flight Centre, how can I help?

   B: Well, I left a message earlier about my flight to Madrid.

c **A:** Patrick? It's Jude Cummins here – sorry it's a bit late.

   B: Oh, thanks for getting back to me, Jude.

d **A:** I'm calling about a mistake on my phone bill.

   B: Sorry to stop you there, I'll have to put you through to another department.

e **A:** Hello, this is Mrs Howard, Dan's mother – you wanted to speak to me.

   B: Yes, it's regarding your son's behaviour at school.

f **A:** The only tickets we have left are at $15 for ...

   B: Sorry, you're breaking up.

g **A:** The wedding menu? Now where did I put it? Should be here somewhere. Oops, now I've dropped everything and ....

   B: Sorry, am I calling at a bad time?

h **A:** Could you check and see when my order was actually sent out?

   B: Sure. Can I just confirm your name and postcode?

i **A:** This is Shoreton's Wholesale Foods. Do you want to order anything this week?

   B: I'm not sure. If you'll just bear with me, I'll ask my boss.

j **A:** We should have somebody with you by three o'clock.

   B: Could you speak up a bit, please?

   A: I said, we should have somebody with you by three.

UNIT 6 RECORDING 1

Greatest Superheroes of All Time

With their simple stories of good versus evil, comic-book superheroes are as popular today as when they first appeared. So, who are these much-loved characters? Here is a brief introduction to four of the greatest superheroes of all.

In 1939 America, DC Comics seized on the public's desire for escapism during a period of social and economic deprivation, and developed a new superhero. The creators of the 'Man of Steel' wanted a hero in a colourful costume who would look good in a comic book. Although there had been superheroes before, this was the first 'total package' with a costume, secret identity and abilities beyond those of mortal men. Born in a far-off galaxy, the baby hero discovers as he grows up that our sun gives him extraordinary powers: he can fly 'faster than a speeding bullet', has incredible strength and X-ray vision, and can only be hurt or destroyed by a green rock from his original planet, Krypton. He is adopted and brought up by Martha and Jonathan Kent to uphold truth, justice and the 'American way'. Whenever danger calls, he is never far from a telephone box and a quick change, ready to save the world. He's had several TV and film incarnations, the most successful of which starred Christopher Reeve and Margot Kidder in 1978. Ironically, creators Siegel and Shuster signed away their rights to the character for $130!

Born on Paradise Island, youthful and immortal, this princess has been blessed by ancient gods and goddesses with powers of super strength and speed and the ability to fly. The superheroine made her first appearance in 1941. It is said she was invented by William Marston for DC Comics as a role model for girls and to raise the morale of US troops in World War II. Her alter-ego, Diana Price, works as a hospital nurse, but transforms herself by flicking her lasso. As well as the lie-detecting lasso, she has bracelets which can stop bullets, but unfortunately she loses her powers if she is tied up with her own lasso. She is instantly recognisable by her stars and stripes costume and in 1976, her adventures were brought to life in a three-year TV series starring ex-Miss USA Beauty Queen, Linda Carter.

Created by artist Bob Kane and writer Bill Finger for DC Comics, the stories combined superheroics and a secret identity. This character cannot stop bullets, fly, or look through walls. He is a normal man who becomes one of the greatest crimefighters ever because of his detective skills, highly-trained physical abilities, amazing gadgets, and of course, his 'batmobile' car, kept in a hidden cave beneath his mansion. By day he is rich socialite Bruce Wayne, but at night he turns into 'the caped crusader', accompanied by his side-kick,

Robin. He was memorably brought to life in the 1960s TV series and in the film of 1996, starring Michael Keaton, Kim Basinger and Jack Nicholson – a film that featured four of the series' best arch-villains: Catwoman, The Joker, The Penguin and The Riddler.

Like many other superheroes, Peter Parker is an orphan, although he has an uncle (Ben) and aunt (Mae). Part of his appeal is that both adolescents and adults can readily identify with him. A poor school student, he goes on to become a regular working guy; a high-school teacher with both girlfriend and money problems. His world is turned upside down when his Uncle Ben is murdered. He gains his superpowers during a high school science demonstration when a radiated spider bites him and gives him superhuman strength and reflexes and the ability to stick to most surfaces. In the movie, which was the biggest money spinner of 2002, Parker grows webslingers which shoot and spin webs, and puts on his red and blue costume to fight arch-enemies such as the Green Goblin and Doctor Octopus.

UNIT 6 RECORDING 2

Have you
Have you lived
Have you lived here long?
How long
How long have you been
How long have you been working here?

UNIT 6 RECORDING 3

1 What have you been doing?
2 How long has she lived there?
3 Have you seen this film before?
4 How long has he been waiting?
5 Have you tried Thai food?
6 Have they finished their homework?
7 How long have you been studying English?
8 Has she been working hard?

UNIT 7 RECORDING 1

1 I get really annoyed by cyclists who ride on the pavement.
2 I hate people who talk loudly on their mobile phones on the train.
3 I hate jeans that are too tight.
4 I really don't like parties where I don't know anyone.
5 I can't stand the taste of cola which has gone flat.
6 I hate days when I don't get anything finished.
7 I really don't like restaurants where the service is slow.
8 I get annoyed by children whose parents let them make a lot of noise.
9 I hate sandwiches that have too much butter in them.
10 I hate politicians whose policies change as soon as they get into power.

UNIT 7 RECORDING 2

Hughie Erskine, who was a charming and attractive young man, was unfortunately not very successful in business and therefore did not have much money. He was in love with a beautiful girl called Laura Merton, whose father had demanded £10,000 to allow them to marry. One day, Hughie went to visit his friend Alan Trevor, who was an artist. Trevor was just putting the finishing touches to a portrait of a beggar. The beggar, who was wearing torn, shabby old clothes and holding out his hat for money, looked sad and tired. 'Poor old man,' thought Hughie, 'he looks so miserable,' and gave the man a pound, which was all the money he had. The beggar smiled and said, 'Thank you sir, thank you.' Hughie spent the rest of the day with Laura, who was annoyed because he had given away his last pound, and he had to walk home because he had no money for a bus. The next day he went to a bar, where he met Alan Trevor. Trevor told him that the 'beggar' was in reality Baron Hausberg, whose financial skills had made him a millionaire. Hughie felt deeply embarrassed about giving him the pound. The following day, he received an envelope from the Baron, which had a cheque for £10,000 inside it . The message on the envelope said: 'A wedding present to Hughie and Laura from an old beggar'.

Audio script

UNIT 7 RECORDING 3

A   I was working as a journalist for a small, independent tech magazine at the time, and we had one invitation to the event – I was lucky enough to be chosen from our office to attend. The atmosphere as you entered the room was electric, everyone was excited and there was a constant buzz of chatter until the lights went out and the opening music came on. There had been rumours circulating as to what it was going to be for a few days, and so people already had a basic idea, but when it was finally revealed, I don't think anyone had expected to see something so well-designed – people were truly 'wowed', and there was an audible pause before everybody clapped and cheered. It was amazing to see just how far we'd come with technology at that point.

B   It was amazing. Everyone was already expecting something special because of who the director was, but this really surpassed our expectations. The fireworks were amazing, but what really topped it off was when the Queen arrived. At that point the crowd went wild, and people near me were waving a bright banner, which read: 'We love you London!' That summed it up for me, I think, as the whole show was a celebration of everything British. It was an excellent start to what turned out to be a fantastic event. The excitement lasted all summer.

C   I was there with my brother, and we had been lucky enough to get tickets at the last minute. We hadn't really expected to get so far in the tournament, and had had to make lots of last-minute arrangements in order to be able to stay there for the match. But it was definitely worth it. Noone actually scored throughout the game, and we were literally on the edge of our seats the whole time. The atmosphere was a strange mix of excitement and exhaustion, as both players and spectators were getting tired. Then, Iniesta came through at the end of extra time and our half of the stadium went wild. It was crazy, people I didn't know were embracing me and shouting – several grown men were crying tears of happiness by the end. At that moment, I felt really proud of the team and my country. As this was the first time we'd won this competition, it really was quite an achievement.

D   At the time I was probably one of the world's biggest fans of the series, so when I heard that I'd won a competition to be one of 1,700 people at a special event at the Natural History Museum, I couldn't believe my luck. This was a special gathering organised by the publisher, in which the author gave a speech, followed by an all-night event during which, at midnight, we all received a free, signed copy of the final book. There were so many unanswered questions from the earlier books in the series, which we were promised would finally be answered in this book. So, although the celebration was really good fun, to be honest, by the end of the night I just wanted to get home and start reading!

UNIT 7 RECORDING 4

1   [politely] I hope I didn't offend you.
    [sarcastically] I hope I didn't offend you.
2   [off-hand] How's everything going?
    [politely] How's everything going?
3   [angrily] Don't worry, it's not important.
    [politely] Don't worry, it's not important.
4   [politely] No, really. I couldn't manage any more.
    [angrily] No, really. I couldn't manage any more.
5   [politely] It doesn't matter. These things happen.
    [angrily] It doesn't matter. These things happen.
6   [politely] I'll call you if I get a chance next week.
    [impatiently] I'll call you if I get a chance next week.

UNIT 7 RECORDING 5

1   I hope I didn't offend you.
2   How's everything going?
3   Don't worry, it's not important.
4   No, really. I couldn't manage any more.
5   It doesn't matter. These things happen.
6   I'll call you if I get a chance next week.

UNIT 8 RECORDING 1

A   I work in a market in London, just at the weekends – I've got a second-hand book stall – and one day I was getting my stall ready, when a lady came up and started looking at the books. She started chatting and telling me how she used to live in that part of London and how much it had changed since she'd last been in the area. While we were talking, I put out a book and she picked it up. 'Oh, Grimm's Fairy Tales,' she said, ' I had a copy of this when I was a child. I used to read it again and again.' She began flicking through it and I carried on laying out the books, and when I looked up she was just standing there shaking, and she'd gone completely white. 'But ... but ... this is my actual book,' she gasped, 'look, it's got my name, Joan, in it. How on earth did you get it?' Then she told me how there'd been a terrible fire while her family were away on holiday, and the house had been burnt to the ground. She thought all her belongings had been destroyed. She pulled out her purse to buy the book from me, but I stopped her. 'No, no ... please accept it as a gift – it's such a wonderful story.'

B   I was walking along the road in Windsor where I live, when I heard a phone ringing in a phone box, and something prompted me to go in and pick it up. There was a voice at the other end saying, in a very business-like way, 'Sorry to bother you at home, Julian, but I can't find that file you were working on. Do you remember where you put it?' It was Jasmine, who I work with at my office in London. I stopped her before she could go on. 'Jasmine, I'm in a phone box – how did you know I was here?' And she just said, 'Stop messing around, I'm really busy and I need that file.' I kept trying to convince her about where I was, but she just wouldn't believe me. Anyway, I told her where the file was, and then suddenly she interrupted me: 'Julian! Hang on a minute – I didn't dial your home phone number! I dialled the Windsor code, but then I dialled your security card number, which is next to your name in the book at work.' So, somehow, my security card number just happened to be the same number as the phone box that I was walking past.

C   A couple of years ago, we moved to an old house in the country, and the man who lived there before had died, and we had to clear up a lot of his belongings. So we built a big bonfire at the end of the garden and took all the rubbish down there to burn. I'd just put a box full of stuff onto the fire, and I was standing chatting, when there was a bang, and I felt something hit the side of my head. I took my earring off and there was a bullet stuck in it, which had been on the fire and had exploded. If I hadn't had the earrings on, it would've gone straight into my neck. And the scary thing was, the bullet had the letter 'J' on it – and my name's Jane – so it was as if this bullet was intended for me!

UNIT 8 RECORDING 2

1   Wear a coat when you go out – it's quite cold for this time of year.
2   I find the idea of bungee jumping very frightening.
    OR
    I find the idea of bungee jumping quite frightening.
    OR
    I find the idea of bungee jumping really frightening.
3   Catherine was absolutely furious about the mess that the children had made.
    OR
    Catherine was really furious about the mess that the children had made.
4   Can you turn your music down, please? It's very noisy.
5   We've been moving house all day – we're absolutely exhausted.
6   Mum, I'm absolutely starving – can I have a burger?
7   Have you seen the new sitcom on ABC? It's really funny.
8   Didn't you take an umbrella? You must be absolutely soaked.

UNIT 8 RECORDING 3

1   Look, the river's frozen! It must have been very cold during the night.
2   A: I think Greg's out. He didn't answer the phone.
    B: But he might not have heard it – he sometimes plays his music very loud.
3   A: Here, I brought you some flowers.
    B: Oh, you shouldn't have done that.

OR

    B: Oh, you didn't have to do that.
4   Sally! Look where you're going when you cross the road. You could have been hit by a car!

    OR

    Sally! Look where you're going when you cross the road. You might have been hit by a car!
5   At school we could learn two languages if we wanted to.
6   A: I'm very sorry I'm late, I got stuck in traffic.

    B: Well you could have called to let us know. We've been waiting for half an hour.

    OR

    B: Well you should have called to let us know. We've been waiting for half an hour.

    A: I was going to phone, but I couldn't find the number.

UNIT 8 RECORDING 4

1   She can't have sent the letter.
2   It must have cost a fortune!
3   You should become an actor.
4   Careful, she might have hit you.
5   It could hurt a bit.
6   We can't have put it in the wrong place.

UNIT 8 RECORDING 5

1   She can't have sent the letter.
2   It must have cost a fortune!
3   Careful, she might have hit you.
4   We can't have put it in the wrong place.

UNIT 9 RECORDING 1

A   A young man asked a rich old man how he had become wealthy. The old man said, 'Well, son, it was 1932 in the depth of the Great Depression. I was down to my last cent. I invested that cent in a golf ball. I spent the day polishing the golf ball and at the end of the day I sold it for two cents. The next morning, I invested that two cents in two golf balls. I spent the entire day polishing them and sold them for four cents. I continued like this for a few weeks and by the end of that time I'd accumulated a hundred dollars. Then my wife's father died and left us three million dollars.'

B   Stewart Montgomery of Glasgow, Scotland was going to bed one night when his wife peered out of the bedroom window and told him he'd left the light on in the garage. Montgomery opened the back door to go and switch off the light but saw that there were two men moving about in the garage.

He phoned the police, who asked, 'Is there actually a burglar in your house?' When he said no, they told him to lock all his doors and stay inside; noone was free at the moment but someone would come when available. Montgomery hung up, waited a minute, and then phoned back. 'Hello. I just called to tell you that there were burglars in my garage. Well, you don't have to worry about them now because I've just shot them both.' Within two minutes, four police cars and an ambulance screeched to a halt outside his house. At least ten police officers rushed into the garage and caught the men red-handed. One of the policemen said to Stewart, 'I thought you said you'd shot them!' 'I thought you said there was noone available!' replied Montgomery.

C   A couple went into an exclusive restaurant in Los Angeles. 'I'm sorry,' said the head waiter, 'there are no tables available.'
'Do you know who I am?' said the man. 'I am Dwayne Wright, the film director.'
'I'd like to help you, Mr Wright, but there are no tables left tonight.'
'I'm certain that if the President came in and asked for a table, there would be one free.'
'Well, I suppose so, ... yes,' said the waiter after a brief pause. 'Yes, there would be a table for the President.'
'Good. I'll take it. The President isn't coming this evening, so I'll have his table!'

UNIT 9 RECORDING 2

1   They were very wealthy and lived in a beautiful mansion.
2   Things were pretty bad; I'd lost my job and my home, and I was down to my last cent.
3   Over the years, we've accumulated an enormous number of books.
4   She peered round the door, hoping he'd gone.
5   After I'd hung up, I regretted being so rude to her.
6   He saw the red traffic light at the last minute and screeched to a halt.
7   The police arrived at the bank and caught the robber red-handed.
8   There was a brief pause and then the audience broke into deafening applause.

UNIT 9 RECORDING 3

J = Jenny   D = Drew
J: Oh Drew, I'm so pleased to see you ...
D: Why? What on earth's all that shouting in the kitchen?
J: It's Simon – he's gone completely mad, because he thinks Anna's seeing someone else.
D: Right, I'm going to stop this ...
J: No, no, no, no, it's far too dangerous! He's got a knife!
D: You don't think he'll use it, do you?
J: I really do think he might, because he's been drinking ... Anna's absolutely terrified.
D: This is ridiculous ... let's try and talk to him.
J: It won't do any good, he's far too drunk.
D: OK then, let's call the police – there's absolutely nothing else we can do.

UNIT 9 RECORDING 4

1   Wow, you look absolutely stunning!
2   What on earth have you two been up to in here?
3   It was Sheila who said those things about you, not me.
4   You're such a lucky guy!
5   I did leave a message for you – you must just have missed it.
6   Who on earth can we find to do it at such short notice?
7   It's going to be far too expensive to hire a band for the wedding.
8   What annoyed me was that he didn't once say 'thank you'.

UNIT 9 RECORDING 5

1   A: Do you mind if we stop at the shop quickly on the way?

    B: That's all right by me, I'm in no hurry.
2   A: I don't think this mouse is working properly.

    B: Let me have a look ... no, there's nothing wrong with it, it just needs cleaning.
3   A: Which hole does this part fit into?

    B: The green one, I think. Yeah, that looks about right.
4   A: Wait, where are you going?

    B: Don't worry, I'll be right back.
5   A: I think I'll just stay in and watch TV.

    B: It's not like you to stay in on a Saturday night. What's wrong?
6   A: Is this skirt supposed to have pockets at the front?

    B: No, you've got it on the wrong way round.
7   A: I can't believe Justyna just spoke to me like that in front of everyone else.

    B: Well, it serves you right for spreading gossip about her in the first place.
8   A: Gary's really quite interesting when you get to know him, isn't he?

    B: Yes, I must admit I was completely wrong about him.
9   A: Let's leave it until later.

    B: No, we need to do it right here, right now.
10 A: Why is Dave so depressed at the moment?

    B: It seems everything's gone wrong for him lately; he lost his job and he's split up with his girlfriend.

Audio script

UNIT 9 RECORDING 6

1 A: Any suggestions?
   B: Why not give them a call?
2 A: Have you ever thought about writing your own book?
   B: That's a really good idea, I hadn't thought of that.
3 A: This TV hasn't worked properly since I bought it.
   B: If I were you, I'd take it back.
4 A: I just wondered if you've got any advice about what I should do?
   B: To be honest, the most important thing is to do what's right.
5 A: You should definitely ask her about it, she might just have forgotten.
   B: Yeah, perhaps you're right.
6 A: Grant can't decide what he wants to do when he leaves school.
   B: I would recommend speaking to a careers counsellor.
7 A: Hello, I'd like some advice about these smart phones, please.
   B: Yes, of course. First things first, I would suggest that you decide which features you want.
8 A: You ought to have a word with your boss about your hours, you know.
   B: I know what you mean, it's just hard to find the right time.

UNIT 10 RECORDING 1

Where's the soap?

It's funny how TV programmes don't always live up to your expectations. I can't tell you how many times I've turned on the 'news', only to be told who the winner of a talent show is or what a celebrity has been wearing. Or the number of 'comedies' which didn't make me laugh. So it comes as no surprise that rarely does a 'soap opera' contain soap or singing, let alone classical singing. So, where is the soap?

In 1930, the manager of a Chicago radio station approached a detergent company in order to get sponsorship for a daily, fifteen-minute drama about a woman who left her job as a speech teacher to work in radio. This was to become *Painted Dreams*, a serial considered to be the first soap opera. The format was so popular that by 1940, radio soap operas made up ninety percent of commercially sponsored daytime radio. The word 'soap' comes from the fact that these programmes were sponsored (and sometimes even produced) by companies which produced domestic cleaning products. They were aimed at housewives, who at that time would be at home.

All soap operas are defined by the fact that their storylines are continuous. Several plots often run at the same time, and each episode usually ends with a 'cliffhanger', an open ending designed to make people want to watch or listen to the next episode. Most soap operas are 'open', in that they never end. Some British soap operas have been on TV since the 1950s, though obviously the characters come and go. However, in Latin America, soap operas tend to be 'closed'. Although they last for months and can have hundreds of episodes, *telenovelas* (as they're called there) do reach a conclusion.

In the Americas, soap operas tend to focus on glamorous and seductive characters with wealthy lifestyles, whereas in the UK and Australia, they tend to be based on the lives of working class people. In both cases, storylines are based around family life, relationships, moral issues and sometimes topical issues. Romance and secret relationships feature heavily, and these can be compared to those of old style paperback romance novels. Plots can often move into bizarre areas, such as in an episode of US soap *Dallas*, where in order to bring back a 'dead' character, it was shown that a previous season had all been a dream of one of the characters. Perhaps not as strange as an Australian soap which had one scene showing a male dog dreaming about the female dog from next door!

UNIT 10 RECORDING 2

1 He told her he loved her.
   [*disbelievingly*] He told her he loved her.
2 [*disbelievingly*] Alex said he'd done his homework but had left it at home.
   Alex said he'd done his homework but had left it at home.
3 [*disbelievingly*] The government said they wouldn't raise taxes.
   The government said they wouldn't raise taxes.
4 The witness said she'd never seen the man before.
   [*disbelievingly*] The witness said she'd never seen the man before.
5 Vanessa told her husband she had to work late that night.
   [*disbelievingly*] Vanessa told her husband she had to work late that night.

6 [*disbelievingly*] Joe said he'd left his wallet at home.
   Joe said he'd left his wallet at home.
7 They told us they'd never been here before.
   [*disbelievingly*] They told us they'd never been here before.
8 [*disbelievingly*] Vicky told us she'd really enjoyed the meal.
   Vicky told us she'd really enjoyed the meal.

UNIT 11 RECORDING 1

1 A: What would you do if you could take six months off work?
   B: If my children were a bit older, I'd take them on a world tour.
2 A: What would you do if you became a world leader?
   B: I'd try to make the gap between rich and poor narrower.
3 A: What part of your body would you change if you could?
   B: My hands – I'd love to have slim, elegant fingers.
4 A: If you had to live on a desert island, what would you take with you?
   B: I think I'd take a camera, so I could record the experience.
5 A: What would you rescue from your home if it was on fire?
   B: I'd save as many of my books as I could.
6 A: If you could change places with anyone, who would you choose?
   B: If it was just for a day, I'd choose a supermodel!
   OR
   B: If it were just for a day, I'd choose a supermodel!
7 A: What would you study if you went back to school?
   B: I'd learn Italian, so I could read all those wonderful, old Italian recipe books.
8 A: What would you do if you only had four weeks to live?
   B: I'd eat and drink anything I wanted!

UNIT 11 RECORDING 2

example, eruption, surface
more, dinosaur
pure, fuel
me, catastrophe
teacher, temperature, ocean
say, radioactive
hot, volcanic
area, nuclear
void, asteroid
no, solar, volcano
silent, scientific, dioxide

UNIT 11 RECORDING 3

Researchers at Harvard University, in the US, studied 8,000 men for 65 years and found those who ate modest amounts of chocolate up to three times a month lived almost a year longer than those who didn't eat any. They concluded this was likely to be because cocoa contains antioxidants called polyphenols, also found in red wine, which prevent the oxidation of harmful cholesterol. Antioxidants are also known to protect against cancer.

Although getting caught in the rain may make you feel cold and uncomfortable, this unpleasant experience will not in itself cause you to catch a virus. As the viruses that cause colds and flu are spread by tiny moisture droplets, you can only catch a cold or flu by:
•   breathing in moisture droplets carrying the viruses (often as a result of an infected person coughing or sneezing near you) or;
•   shaking hands with or touching an infected person.
More people seem to catch colds and flu in cold weather because they spend a lot of time indoors together and are therefore more likely to come into contact with viruses. Make sure you wash your hands frequently and stand back from people with coughs and sneezes.

It depends on whether you are referring to the loose product or the brewed cup. Tea leaves have more caffeine than coffee beans before they are brewed. Prepared, however, tea is diluted quite a bit more than most coffees: a pound of tea yields 200–250 cups of tea, while a pound of coffee makes approximately 80 cups. This will of course vary depending on how strong you like your tea or coffee. It has also been found that about 80 percent of the caffeine content in tea is extracted during the first minute of brewing. So if you want to reduce your caffeine intake, one suggestion is to discard the first brew and then make another cup using the same teabag or tea leaves.

A dog may be a man's best friend, but not if the man is among the estimated 10 to 15 percent of the population that suffers from pet allergies. The allergen is a specific protein produced not in the animal's fur, but primarily in its skin and – to a lesser extent – its saliva. As the animal is stroked or brushed, or as it rubs up against furniture or people, microscopic flakes of skin (called dander) become airborne. Since all cats and dogs have skin, there are no non-allergenic breeds. However, since short-haired pets have less hair to shed, they send less dander into the air, so are preferable for those with pet allergies. Dogs are half as likely to cause allergic reactions as cats, but if you're allergic to furry animals, the only no-risk pets are fish and reptiles.

There are all kinds of popular theories: that first thing in the morning is best because you will speed up your metabolism and burn more calories all day; that exercising before dinner will reduce your appetite; that exercise in the evening won't work because it will rev you up and keep you from getting a good night's sleep. However, many experts agree that our body temperature plays an enormous part in exercise and fitness performance, and that the body performs best when its temperature is naturally higher, which is at around six p.m. Muscular temperature also affects our flexibility and strength, so we are less likely to injure ourselves at that time of day, and more likely to be able to develop a muscular physique.

UNIT 12 RECORDING 1

5 steps to making a viral video

Have you ever uploaded a funny or interesting video clip to a video sharing website? Chances are that if you did, it got viewed by some of your friends who you showed it to, but not many people picked up on it from outside your social circle. So what is it that makes some videos go viral? Why do some videos get viewed several million times, especially when they look like they've been put together by a bored teenager at home, with nothing better to do? I spoke to Danika Holmes, a social media analyst with a special interest in video, to ask her advice on what to do if I wanted to make a viral video. Here's what she said.

1   Think about who will be watching your video so you know who to aim it at. Even if you're going for universal appeal, you need to start with a specific, targeted viewer base. Think about what makes these types of people tick and what they like to talk about with their friends.

2   Once you've got to know your audience, you'll need to choose the right entertainment aspect to hit a nerve – the right spark. The four most common sparks are funny, sexy, surprising and random. Cute often makes an appearance as well, but this can have limited appeal to some audiences.

3   Once you've chosen the spark, you need to focus on this aspect and emphasise it. There's no point in your video being 'quite' funny – it's all or nothing. As a general rule, your video should be able to cause a physical reaction such as laughter, crying, a shocked expression, etc.

4   A meme is an iconic symbol of a culture at a specific time, which gets passed on from person to person. This is exactly what you want to happen to your video, so create a buzz, and turn up the volume. Share comments on it on microblogging and social networking websites and encourage other people to do the same.

5   This is the true test of whether your video has gone viral. If people copy your video, wearing different clothes, or acting it out in different situations, or remix to a different soundtrack, then you know you've created a viral video. At the height of the Harlem Shake meme in early 2013, 4,000 copies were being uploaded a day around the world. This also ensures your viral video will be remembered in years to come. And in today's fast-paced, throw-away society, that's quite an achievement.

UNIT 12 RECORDING 2

1   It's important not to focus too much on the negative aspects. Think about the positives, too.
2   I've often wondered what it would be like to be locked up in a house for twelve weeks with nine strangers.
3   One thing I love about weekends is not being woken up by an alarm clock.
4   Despite having done a lot of charity work in his life, he is best remembered for his music.
5   Marsha says she likes not being responsible for other people in her new job, but I don't really believe her.
6   I expected you to have finished that hours ago: why is it taking so long?
7   I don't want to worry you, but there's a huge, black rain cloud over there and it seems to be coming towards us.
8   I'd like to have learnt more about ancient Greek philosophy when I was at university.

UNIT 12 RECORDING 3

1   She agreed to be interviewed.
2   You should focus on winning the race.
3   We'd like to have known about it sooner.
4   I hate being told what to do.
5   You promised not to be late.
6   I want to be lying on a beach right now.

Answer key

UNIT 1

1

2 g   3 a   4 h   5 f   6 d   7 b   8 e

2

2 What are you cooking? It smells wonderful!
3 A lot of people believe he's very talented but I don't agree.
4 A: Why are you being so friendly today?
  B: I'm just in a good mood!
5 Do you know Ken? He's very interesting. He works at the Science Museum.
6 I'm reading this great book. It's about growing up during the 1960s.

3

2 came   3 did you stop   4 were just discussing   5 did, happen
6 didn't you tell   7 thought   8 were just trying

4

2 b   3 b   4 a   5 b   6 b

5

2 Can you smell   3 don't remember   4 do you think
5 doesn't own   6 'm having   7 seems   8 don't like

6

2 ~~used to be~~ was   3 ~~used~~ use   4 ~~be hating~~ hate
5 ~~They've~~ They   6 ~~used you~~ did you use   7 ~~used to go~~ went
8 ~~had~~ used, to

7

2 saw   3 had heard / 'd heard   4 had written
5 didn't know   6 had forgotten / 'd forgotten   7 had left / 'd left
8 had already seen / 'd already seen

8

2 was celebrating   3 got   4 went
5 had received / 'd received   6 has worked / 's worked
7 are / 're   8 has never had   9 didn't have
10 worked   11 has become   12 lived
13 managed   14 has just written   15 is visiting
16 is spending

9b

2 Robert / Claire   3 Robert   4 Rodrigo
5 Claire   6 Celine   7 Robert
8 Robert / Claire

10

2 a   3 a   4 c   5 b   6 a   7 c   8 a

11

2 lie   3 confide in   4 trust   5 behind her back
6 told the truth   7 kept their promises   8 gossip

12

2 d   Ben does look well. Has he been on holiday?
3 a   I do hate it when people are late for meetings.
4 c   We didn't like the hotel, but we did enjoy the tours.
5 b   I do like fish generally, but I don't like it raw.

13

2 Has she? How long has she had it?
3 Aren't you? Why not?
4 Hasn't he? I hope he enjoys it.
5 Do you? I don't.
6 Wasn't there? It's OK, I've got some chicken.

14

2 Well, John has, but Trevor and Ann haven't.   3 Yes, I am, actually.
4 Yes, it does, for two hours.   5 I think it has, but I'll check for you.
6 No, it wasn't, but it was very cold.

15a

2 U, S   3 U, S   4 S, S   5 S   6 U, S

16

2 got, flight   3 gets, tired   4 used to get, presents
5 Did you get, message   6 got, work   7 've got, over
8 got, angry

17

2 Try not to worry about it.   3 Don't take any notice of them.
4 There's no point in getting upset about it.
5 That sounds awful!   6 You must be really worried.
7 Cheer up!   8 Calm down!
9 Just ignore him.   10 How annoying!
11 Don't worry, it doesn't matter.   12 What a shame!

18a

2 d   3 c   4 i   5 g   6 h   7 a   8 e   9 b   10 f

UNIT 2

1a

2 positive   3 panicky   4 upset
5 depressed   6 curious   7 amused
8 grumpy   9 sleepy

1b

1 sleepy   2 upset   3 depressed
4 panicky   5 grumpy   6 amused
7 positive   8 insecure   9 curious

2a

3 secure   4 insecure   5 efficient
6 inefficient   7 successful   8 unsuccessful
9 solved   10 unsolved   11 enthusiastic
12 unenthusiastic   13 comfortable   14 uncomfortable
15 patient   16 impatient   17 honest
18 dishonest

2c

2 uncomfortable   3 patient   4 unsuccessful
5 insecure   6 honest   7 unsolved
8 enthusiastic

3

P	U	R	Y	A	V	E	E	S	G	R	T
U	R	O	S	N	P	O	P	E	P	P	D
N	O	N	S	T	O	P	R	M	R	O	I
D	I	S	T	I	O	U	E	P	O	S	S
E	N	D	R	C	R	E	F	A	D	T	S
R	T	S	E	L	K	O	L	T	E	G	A
C	R	R	S	O	I	L	I	O	M	R	T
O	V	E	S	C	R	I	G	R	O	A	I
O	R	V	E	K	W	Y	H	T	C	D	S
K	R	E	D	W	A	H	T	Y	R	U	F
E	P	A	N	I	C	K	Y	E	A	A	I
D	R	I	O	S	U	N	S	A	C	T	E
S	E	L	F	E	M	P	L	O	Y	E	D

2 panicky 3 stressed 4 dissatisfied
5 self-employed 6 anti-clockwise 7 pro-democracy
8 pre-flight 9 postgraduate 10 undercooked

4

2 bored 3 frustrating 4 fascinated
5 exciting 6 interesting 7 disappointed
8 depressing

5a

B 2   C 3   D 2   E 1   F 3

5b

1 *It's a Wonderful Life* and *Pay it Forward*
2 *Raiders of the Lost Ark* and *Star Wars*
3 *Jaws* and *Jurassic Park*

6

2 h   3 g   4 k   5 j   6 f
7 i   8 d   9 b   10 a   11 l
12 c

7

2 trainee 3 childhood 4 evidence
5 guitarist 6 bottle opener 7 admission
8 Communism 9 community 10 enjoyment
11 nervousness 12 vegetarian

8a

2 eating 3 not drinking 4 not taking
5 getting 6 not talking 7 drinking
8 taking 9 not going 10 not eating

8b

1 1 sleepy 2 upset 3 depressed 4 panicky 5 grumpy
  6 amused 7 positive 8 insecure 9 curious
2 Making new friends is easy for me.
3 I hate people dropping their rubbish in the street.
4 Starting a new job can be very stressful.
5 My mother-in-law can't stand people smoking when she's eating.
6 I find that having a nice long bath is a good way to relax.

9
A

2 anxiety 3 insecurity 4 unemployed
5 exhaustion 6 behaviour 7 criticism
8 confidence

B

2 development 3 investigation 4 Scientists
5 moderation 6 multi-tasking 7 solving
8 leadership 9 decisions 10 reality
11 loneliness

10

•●••	●•••	•●••	●••
reality	pessimism	aggression	loneliness
relationship	criticism	contentment	violence
economist		conformist	

11a
Summary 2

11b

2 panicky 3 impatient 4 frustrating
5 cheerful 6 sociable 7 exhausted

UNIT 3

1a

2 tripped 3 spilt 4 had lost
5 overslept 6 got confused 7 got on
8 dropped 9 damaged 10 broke down
11 slipped 12 banged my head 13 ran out of petrol
14 locked myself out 15 got stuck 16 missed

1b

2 'll spill 3 missed 4 slipped
5 're getting on / 've got on 6 get stuck
7 got lost 8 've run out of 9 get confused
10 overslept 11 dropped 12 banged
13 tripped 14 'd locked herself out 15 Has, lost
16 damage

2

2 We were walking around a town when a man offered to change our money.
3 A friend had warned us never to change money on the street, but the man looked honest, so we decided to take a chance.
4 He pretended to give me fifty notes but I noticed that he had only given me forty-eight, so I asked him to count them again.
5 Ten minutes later we were sitting in a café when I realised that he had tricked us.
6 When he gave me back the money, he had replaced everything except the top two notes with newspaper!

3

2 had drunk 3 had resigned 4 had been going out
5 hadn't come 6 'd been working 7 'd been trying
8 hadn't paid

4

2 tried 3 had been looking forward
4 had made 5 went 6 was having
7 cut 8 had been doing 9 hadn't won
10 showed 11 couldn't 12 were planning
13 told 14 'd made 15 didn't speak

5

2 possession (of) illegal drugs 3 played truant
4 anti-social behaviour 5 graffiti 6 begging

6

2 taken into care, given community service, C
3 lost his licence, got a suspended sentence, A

7

2 has been growing 3 has been feeling 4 haven't had
5 've never held 6 have died 7 've never used
8 've been thinking 9 've decided

8

2 'll be 3 'll be wandering 4 'll be having
5 won't be working 6 'll send 7 'll bring
8 will be looking after 9 won't forget 10 'll phone

9

2 've been staying 3 'll go out 4 have you been doing
5 'll be giving 6 've said 7 's won
8 'll be taking

10

2 set to, f 3 back, e 4 Death toll, a
5 calls, d 6 vows, b

Answer key

11a

The Italian lottery syndicate

11b

| 1 F | 2 F | 3 T | 4 F | 5 F | 6 T |

11c

2   Krista Saputo.
3   Vincenzo Paviglianiti or other members of the syndicate.
4   Wan Song's husband, Inhong Song.   5   Eric Culbertson.
6   The Italian police.   7   Wan Song.
8   The five masked gunmen.

12a

2   it's not (my) fault   3   understand that
4   make (a) suggestion? (Why) don't (I)   5   think (that's) fair
6   this (is) ridiculous

13

| 2 b, a | 3 b, a | 4 a, b | 5 b, a | 6 a, b |

14a

B is true.

14b

Several years ago I was spending Christmas in Tenerife, in the Canary Islands. My brother José was working there and **unfortunately** he couldn't get any time off to come home, so I spent the holiday with him. **One day** we decided to go up Mount Teide, a volcano in the centre of the island. This was the last day of my visit, so we hired a little car for the day.

José and I set off in brilliant sunshine, but **very quickly** it got much colder and by the time we reached the crater of Mount Teide it was snowing. **For some reason** all the restaurants, hotels and petrol stations at the top of the volcano were shut, and we had almost run out of petrol. **At this point,** I started getting really worried because I had to catch the plane home that evening, and if I didn't, I would have to pay for a new ticket. So José decided to do something incredibly dangerous – he switched off the engine of the car and freewheeled down the other side of the mountain. He did this for several kilometres, round hairpin bends on dangerous, icy roads. I was absolutely petrified, but for some reason I didn't tell him to stop. **All of sudden** my worst nightmare happened: the car slipped on the road and the two front wheels went over the edge. We were very lucky that the rest of the car didn't go over. We sat in the car **for ages**, not daring to move and freezing cold, waiting for someone to come past. **Eventually,** a car came round the corner and out jumped three enormous men. Without saying a word, the three men surrounded the car and literally lifted it back on the road. My brother and I got out to thank them, but the three men just repeated 'Norway' several times – we assumed that that was where they came from – then got back into their car and drove off. **By this stage** we were so relieved we could have kissed them! We got back into our car and continued down the side of the mountain. I have never felt so happy in my life as when we reached the town at the bottom. We went straight to a petrol station and filled up. **Ironically,** the petrol station was owned by a Norwegian company!

UNIT 4

1

2   visual/spatial intelligence   3   memory
4   musical ability   5   emotional intelligence
6   organisational skills   7   creativity and imagination
8   problem-solving skills

2

2   the Taj Mahal   3   the television   4   football
5   Barack Obama   6   London

3a

2   is spoken, b Brazil
3   has been known, b sixty years
4   a tablets, are being bought
5   was (originally) inhabited, b Maoris
6   will not be held / won't be held, a Brazil
7   had (already) arrived, b 1492
8   was played, b Daniel Craig

4

Text A

2   need   3   are specially formulated / have been specially formulated
4   contains   5   not be taken

Text B

1   has only recently opened   2   are offering
3   includes   4   is limited
5   be made

Text C

1   has been used   2   was believed
3   was used   4   believed
5   protect

Text D

1   was being investigated   2   complained
3   had not been properly cleaned   4   are currently being treated
5   to be sent

5

| 2 b | 3 a | 4 a | 5 a |
| 6 b | 7 b | 8 a | |

6c

| 2 T | 3 F | 4 F | 5 T | 6 T | 7 F |
| 8 T | 9 T | 10 T | 11 F | 12 T | |

7

2   She's very tolerant. She's quite open-minded about things.
3   I'm sorry. I'm not very good company this evening. I've got something on my mind.
4   Has Mrs Chen changed her mind? I thought she was staying at the Hilton.
5   Although I'd met Vladimir several times before, my mind went blank and I couldn't remember his name.
6   You've lost my pen? Oh, never mind. It wasn't valuable.
7   Would you mind helping me with my suitcases?
8   Dave is so absent-minded. He got all the way to the theatre and then realised he'd got the wrong date.
9   I made (up) my mind (up) not to take the job.
10   Mind the gap between the train and the platform.
11   Yes, I got a pay rise, but no, I'm not going to tell you how much. Mind your own business!
12   My new secretary is surprisingly honest. She certainly speaks her mind.

8

2 Have you ever had your hair dyed?
3 When did you last get your eyes tested?
4 Have you ever had your photo taken with someone famous?
5 Would you like to have your hair cut differently?
6 Has your house ever been broken into?

9a

2 Yes, I've finally got an article published in the local newspaper!
3 Can you have these business cards printed for me?
4 I'd have it checked by a lawyer, if I were you.
5 No, I'll pay for you to get it cleaned.
6 We're having some shelves put up.

10

Sarah: rebellious
Juan: extrovert, hot-tempered
Maria: good in a team, calm
Laura: arrogant, attention-seeking
Jim: introvert, needy

11

P	S	F	T	K	S	S	R	I	E	J	T	V	E	E
C	O	M	U	T	H	S	S	N	I	U	O	W	X	E
Q	U	E	R	K	U	M	U	D	A	T	I	O	P	R
U	N	C	O	M	M	U	N	I	C	A	T	I	V	E
W	E	E	Y	P	O	R	V	V	M	E	I	O	D	S
J	E	A	L	O	U	S	E	I	Y	Z	J	E	R	I
H	O	D	T	F	R	Y	J	D	S	T	R	E	I	L
A	E	D	D	U	L	P	L	U	D	E	R	S	W	I
A	R	G	U	M	E	N	T	A	T	I	V	E	E	E
E	D	J	D	R	S	C	G	L	Y	K	G	S	S	N
P	O	T	E	R	S	W	U	I	A	U	A	A	B	T
I	N	R	T	R	E	P	A	S	D	E	W	O	N	E
S	E	L	T	A	L	K	A	T	I	V	E	I	V	E
S	E	L	F	S	U	F	F	I	C	I	E	N	T	G
E	J	L	Y	M	D	T	H	C	U	E	G	H	D	R

2 uncommunicative   3 argumentative   4 talkative
5 self-sufficient   6 humourless   7 individualistic
8 resilient

12a

●●●● rebellious resilient	●●●●● uncommunicative	●●●● creativity argumentative
●● logic needy spatial	●●● extrovert humorous talkative	●●●●● absent-minded open-minded self-sufficient

13a

2 hectic   3 logic   4 needy
5 humourless   6 don't really mind   7 made up my mind
8 give my love to Grandma

UNIT 5

1a

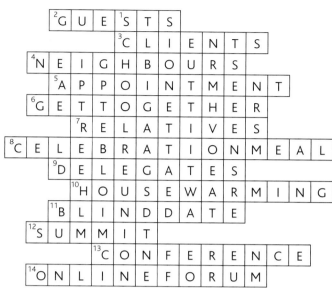

2

2 'll lend   3 'm going to have   4 'll send
5 're going to paint   6 'm going to work   7 'll think
8 're not going to sell   9 'll check
10 'm never going to speak

3

3 ~~really enjoying~~   7 ~~meeting~~   8 ~~making~~   10 ~~learning~~

4

2 Everything on the menu sounds delicious, but **I'll / I'm going to** have the chicken risotto.
3 **You'll / You're going to** break that window if you're not careful.
5 Wait a minute – **I'll** help you with those bags.
6 As soon as I get home, I promise **I'll** phone you.

5 a and b

2 going to; S   3 going to; R   4 I'm sure; R
5 may well; R   6 I'm sure; S
7 there's a good chance that; R   8 almost certainly; S
9 are likely; R   10 certain to; S

6a

2 Lynn and Andy
3 Ben
4 Lukas

6b

1 a   2 b   3 b   4 b   5 b
6 a   7 b   8 b

7

b What's up   c Wanna   d grab a coffee
e gonna   f totally stressed out   g How come
h doing my head in   i was like   j chill out
k mate   l A tenner   m a rip off

8

2 with a pinch of salt   3 be economical with the truth
4 tell a few little white lies   5 fall helplessly in love

Answer key

UNIT 6

9

2 How well   3 How far   4 What benefits
5 How long   6 Which operating system
7 What food   8 How expensive

10

2 Who are you talking to?   3 What are you frightened of?
4 Which one did you apply for?   5 What are you thinking about?
6 Who do you play with?

11

2 c, Don't   3 e, Can't   4 d, Haven't
5 f, Didn't   6 b, Isn't

12

2 I wonder if she liked her present.
3 Tell me what time you want to leave.
4 Do you know where the guided tour leaves from?
5 Can you remind me what time we have to get up tomorrow?
6 They wanted to know whether I was going to the party.
7 Can you tell me what time it is?
8 Do you know how much this costs?

13

2 Q   3 Q   4 S   5 Q
6 Q   7 S   8 Q

14

2 I left a message (earlier) about my flight to Madrid (earlier). b
3 Sorry – you're breaking up. f
4 I'll have to put you through to another department. d
5 Sorry, am I calling at a bad time? g
6 Could you speak up a bit, please? j
7 thanks for getting back to me, Jude. c
8 If you'll just bear with me, I'll ask my boss. i
9 Can I just confirm your name and postcode? h
10 it's regarding your son's behaviour at school. e

15a

2 g   3 e   4 a   5 f   6 d   7 b

15b

Email A is formal   Email B is informal   Email C is semi-formal

15c

2 suitable   3 Hey/Hi
4 our treat   5 Can't wait to see you
6 I'm really delighted for you   7 By the way
8 I'm really looking forward to seeing you   9 Can't wait to see you!

1

1 Superman   2 Wonder Woman   3 Batman   4 Spiderman

2

1 He was a 'total package' with a costume, secret identity, and abilities beyond those of mortal men.
2 Our sun.
3 He can be hurt or destroyed by a green rock from his original planet, Krypton.
4 Superman's adoptive mother.
5 Ancient gods and goddesses.
6 As a role model for girls and to raise the morale of US troops in World War II.
7 A second identity.
8 Transform her into Wonder Woman, detect lies and take away her powers (if she is tied up with it).
9 He is a normal man with no superhuman powers.
10 Bruce Wayne.
11 Robin.
12 They died.
13 No, he gained them during a high school science demonstration.
14 He can stick to most surfaces, and can shoot and spin webs using his webslingers.

3

2 have lost, have   3 be, have done   4 have had, give
5 have visited, feel

4

2 Have you finished your homework yet?
3 I've never tried Ethiopian food.
4 She's been at that school since January.
5 Have you ever read any Bukowski?
6 Many scientists fear we've already passed the tipping point for climate change.
7 Good timing! I've just made fresh coffee.
8 Tratorie's scored 23 goals so far this season.
9 How long has it been? I haven't seen you for years!
10 What have you done today?

5

2 had provided   3 switched (it) off   4 had moved
5 had previously been   6 went   7 had developed
8 became   9 used

6

2 d; 've   3 g; won't have   4 f; have
5 h; will you have   6 a; hadn't   7 e; Have
8 b; 'd

7

2 won   3 set   4 speeches
5 become   6 written   7 founded
8 gave

8a

2 invented   3 set   4 won
5 founded   6 wrote   7 discovered
8 gave

8b

2 b   3 a   4 a   5 b   6 a   7 b   8 a

9a

2 He's one of the bravest ... people I know.   3 In the 1960s
4 it took him years to   5 One   6 Eventually
7 As a result of his actions   8 It's incredible to think that

10

1 've only managed   2 've been making, 've lost
3 've failed, 've been studying   4 've been looking, 've only found
5 've been waking up, 've tried
6 's been behaving, 's started, 's stopped

11

3 ~~He's been collecting~~ He's collected
4 ~~It's snowed.~~ It's been snowing.
5 ~~still have finished~~ still haven't finished
7 ~~We've waited~~ We've been waiting
9 ~~I've always been loving~~ I've always loved

12b

2 How long has she lived there?
3 Have you seen this film before?
4 How long has he been waiting?
5 Have you tried Thai food?
6 Have they finished their homework?
7 How long have you been studying English?
8 Has she been working hard?

13

2 At first   3 at first sight   4 first language
5 first aid   6 First of all   7 first thing
8 first choice   9 first impression   10 in first place

UNIT 7

1

2 parade   3 marcher   4 demonstration
5 crowd   6 protester   7 chant
8 supporter   9 clash   10 flag
11 wave   12 wild   13 carnival
14 placard   15 cheer

2a

2 g   3 e   4 a   5 h   6 i
7 d   8 c   9 f   10 b

3b

Hughie Erskine, **who was a charming and attractive young man**, was unfortunately not very successful in business and therefore did not have much money. He was in love with a beautiful girl called Laura Merton, **whose father had demanded £10,000 to allow them to marry**. One day Hughie went to visit his friend Alan Trevor, **who was an artist**. Trevor was just putting the finishing touches to a portrait of a beggar. The beggar, **who was wearing torn, shabby old clothes and holding out his hat for money**, looked sad and tired. 'Poor old man,' thought Hughie, 'he looks so miserable,' and gave the man a pound, **which was all the money he had**. The beggar smiled and said, 'Thank you, sir, thank you.' Hughie spent the rest of the day with Laura, **who was annoyed because he had given away his last pound**, and he had to walk home because he had no money for a bus. The next day he went to a bar, **where he met Alan Trevor**. Trevor told him that the 'beggar' was in reality Baron Hausberg, **whose financial skills had made him a millionaire**. Hughie felt deeply embarrassed about giving him the pound. The following day he received an envelope from the Baron, **which had a cheque for £10,000 inside it**. The message on the envelope said: 'A wedding present to Hughie and Laura from an old beggar'.

4

1 This version, which includes new special effects, is a 'must' for all Arnie fans.
2 *The Comedy Collection*, which features the brilliant Steve Jones and newcomer Martin Simons, finishes on Friday. Tickets, which cost $18 and $30, are available on the door.
3 'Old New York' opens this weekend at the Brinkley Gallery, which has recently reopened. This exhibition of photographs, which took six months to put together, takes you through fifty years of New York's history.

5a

2 A   3 D   4 B

5b

2 T   3 F   4 F   5 T   6 T   7 F
8 F   9 T   10 T   11 F   12 F

6a

2 d   3 f   4 b   5 a   6 e   7 g

6b

a speech   b headline, stage   c stalls, balloons
d float, costumes   e coffin, mourners   f guests, presents
g parade, fireworks

7

2 We know quite **a** few of our neighbours, but not all of them.
3 We had a lot **of** fun learning to scuba dive today.
4 I think we'll have plenty of glasses for everyone.
5 There are a number **of** reasons why the President resigned.
6 There was too much food for four people to eat.
7 Over fifty people applied for the job, but very few of them had the right qualifications.
8 There's a little space for an extra chair here.
9 There are only a few places where you can buy this type of cheese.
10 As any doctor will tell you, you should eat a balanced diet.

8

2 quite a few   3 plenty   4 a great deal of
5 too much   6 enough   7 very few
8 any   9 plenty of   10 too much
11 some   12 very little   13 too much
14 a number of   15 any   16 a few
17 very few   18 any   19 too many

Answer key

9

2 does it take	3 take care of	4 took notes
5 I take after	6 took place	7 took up
8 take part		

10a

2 g	3 d, relaxed	4 a
5 f, routine	6 c, new	7 e, fan

11

2 b I couldn't possibly manage any more.
3 d I'm afraid I can't eat prawns.
4 c How lovely to see you again.
5 a It doesn't matter in the slightest.

12a

2 B	3 B	4 A	5 A	6 A

UNIT 8

1

2 h	3 a	4 j	5 b	6 g
7 e	8 i	9 d	10 f	11 k

2a

A2	B4	C3

2b

2 C	3 B	4 A	5 C	6 A	7 A
8 C	9 A	10 C	11 B	12 B	

2c

2 through (Text A line 10)	3 gone (Text A line 12)
4 around (Text B line 10)	5 dialled (Text B line 15)
6 happened (Text B line 18)	7 up (Text C line 3)
8 stuff (Text C line 5)	9 stuck (Text C line 7)

3

2 mustn't	3 might	4 shouldn't, could
5 can't	6 can't	7 have to	8 could

4

2 You must / You have to
3 It can't, There must be / There has to be
4 I should / I ought to
5 I mustn't / I can't
6 We might / We may
7 You don't have to
8 he might be / he may be
9 you shouldn't / you oughtn't to
10 Can I / Could I / May I, I have to

5

2 might / could / may	3 should	4 can't
5 don't have to	6 Can / May	7 must

6

2 ridiculous	3 huge	4 deafening	5 superb
6 exhausting	7 tiny	8 stunning	9 horrendous
10 starving			

7a

2 very/quite/really/extremely	3 absolutely/really
6 starving	8 soaked

8a

---

2 couldn't hear, may have heard   3 couldn't have done
4 must have been   5 had to learn, managed to learn
6 must have called/can't have found, couldn't have found

9

A

1 Where did you last have it?
2 I don't know. I used it last night when I bought a/my train ticket, so I must have had it then.
3 Have you used it since then?
4 No. I suppose I might have lost it on the train or I might have left it at home this morning.
5 Why don't you phone home and/to check?

B

1 Where have you been? It's eleven o'clock!
2 I got stuck in (the/some) traffic.
3 Well, you should have phoned!
4 I'm sorry, I left my mobile phone at home.
5 But if I'd known you were going to be late (you'd be late), I could have gone to the pub.
6 I'm really sorry.

10

2 must have been
3 must have gone
4 should have thrown / ought to have thrown / could have thrown
5 must have had
6 should have told / ought to have told / might have told / could have told
7 might have eaten / could have eaten
8 might have been / could have been
9 can't have read (seen) / couldn't have read (seen) / might not have read (seen)
10 shouldn't have eaten / oughtn't to have eaten

11a

2 a	3 b	4 a	5 b	6 a

12

2 screams	3 fortress	4 aliens	5 UFO
6 gunshot wounds	7 lie detector	8 abduction	
9 nailed shut	10 hover		

13a

Adjectives	Mysteries and oddities	Objects/places
alone	coincidence	bolts
awful	hoax	carriage
cold	phenomenon	dark, empty road
deafening	practical joke	golden disc
frightened	supernatural event	iron bars
huge	unexplained natural	key
incredible	unfortunate mishap	medicine
massive		prescription for
quiet		ship
stormy		small box
stunning		
tiny		
tired		

UNIT 9

1a

A How to make money   B How to get the attention of the police
C How to get a table at a restaurant

1b

2 The waiter   3 Stewart Montgomery   4 The waiter
5 The rich old man   6 Dwayne Wright

1c

2 was down to my last cent   3 accumulated   4 peered
5 hung up   6 screeched to a halt   7 red-handed
8 brief pause

2

2 looked up to   3 saw through   4 stand out
5 stand up   6 making (it) up

3

An old man was backing **a** BMW into **a** parking space when **a** bright red sports car drove in behind him and took **the** space. **A** young man jumped out and said, 'Sorry, old man, but you've got to be young and fast to do that.' **The** old man ignored **the** young man and kept reversing until **the** BMW had destroyed **the** sports car completely. 'Sorry, son, you've got to be old and rich to do that!'

4

1b The traffic   2a the exercise   2b Exercise   3a people
3b the people   4a music   4b The music   5a The poetry
5b poetry

5

2 –   3 –   4 –   5 the
6 the   7 the   8 –

6

1b ✓   2a ✓   2b a   3a the   3b ✓
4a ✓   4b the (church)   5a the   5b ✓

7

2 –   3 a   4 a/the   5 The   6 –   7 –
8 a   9 –   10 –   11 the   12 the   13 A
14 –   15 –   16 –   17 –   18 The   19 –
20 an   21 the   22 –

8

2 lose (the) weight and cope with the stress of modern life.
3 Here are (the) some tips for finding the best gym for you.
4 ✓
5 Check for (the) cleanliness, especially in the changing rooms.
6 ✓
7 requirements. Expect (the) well-qualified, presentable instructors.
8 ✓
9 for (an) assistance. Is the club security-conscious – do you need
10 ✓
11 ✓
12 a short distance away – if it takes you more than (the) thirty minutes
13 ✓

9

1 At Christmas my mother usually goes to church at eight o'clock, then she comes home and cooks a huge lunch.
2 Deborah left home last year – now she works / 's working as a lecturer in Vancouver.
3 I visited Uncle Frank in hospital yesterday morning. He's very lucky, because he's got one of the best heart specialists in the UK.

4 A: Is Jamie happy at school?
   B: Yes. He likes the teachers, and the school is only five minutes away, in Kilmorie Road.
5 Gordon is a terrible cook. He invited us for dinner last Saturday evening and it was one of the worst meals I've ever had.

10a

JENNY: Oh Drew, I'm **so** pleased to see you …

DREW: Why? What **on earth**'s all that shouting in the kitchen?

JENNY: It's Simon – he's gone **completely** mad, because he thinks Anna's seeing someone else.

DREW: (*walking towards the kitchen*) Right, I'm going to stop this …

JENNY: (*running after him and pulling him back*) No, it's **far too** dangerous! He's got a knife!

DREW: You don't think he'll use it, do you?

JENNY: I **really do** think he might, because he's been drinking … Anna's **absolutely** terrified.

DREW: (*walking around agitatedly*) This is ridiculous … let's try and talk to him.

JENNY: It won't do any good, he's **far too** drunk.

DREW: (*picking up the phone*) OK then, let's call the police – there's **absolutely** nothing else we can do.

11

2 Susan does like you, she's just a bit shy.
3 Don't be such a baby!
4 Where on earth have you been?
5 Jamie's party was absolutely fantastic.
6 Thomas does know how to get what he wants!
7 The traffic (on that route) is always completely horrendous (on that route).
8 It was such a boring film that I fell asleep before the end.
9 It was Jenny/me who borrowed your jacket, not me/Jenny.
10 Why on earth would you say that to her?

12a

2 earth   3 Sheila   4 such   5 did
6 earth   7 far   8 annoyed

13a

2 e there's nothing wrong with it   3 a that looks about right
4 h I'll be right back   5 d What's wrong?
6 b the wrong way round   7 j it serves you right
8 i I was completely wrong about him
9 f right here, right now   10 c everything's gone wrong

14a

2 thought; hadn't   3 were; 'd
4 should; important   5 definitely; perhaps
6 would; speaking   7 advice; suggest
8 ought; mean

15a

2 enquire   3 currently   4 looking   5 its
6 exactly the type   7 enclosed   8 grateful
9 would consider   10 require   11 hearing
12 faithfully

Answer key

UNIT 10

1

```
 2P R O D U 1C T
              3C O V E R A G E
          4R E A D E R S H I P
              5I N T E R A C T I V E
        6S O A P O P E R A
          7B R O A D S H E E T
                8U P L O A D
    9M I C R O B L O G G I N G
      10S C R E E N T I M E
  11S O C I A L M E D I A
        12M A S S M E D I A
      13A U D I E N C E
                    14T A B L O I D
      15D R A M A S E R I E S
```

2	product	3	coverage	4 readership	5 interactive
6	soap opera	7	broadsheet	8 upload	9 microblogging
10	screen time	11	social media	12 mass media	13 audience
14	tabloid	15	drama series		

2a

1, 3, 4, 6, 8, 9

2b

1 T   2 F (It was about a woman who used to be a teacher.)
3 F (ninety percent of commercially sponsored, daytime programmes.)
4 T   5 F (A 'cliffhanger' is an open ending to an episode which leaves you wanting to find out what happens next.)
6 T   7 T   8 F (They tend to be working class.)
9 F (Romance features heavily in soap operas and in old style paperback novels.)   10 T

3a

1, 2, 4, 6 (in some cultures) and 8 are compliments

3b

2 I admire your honesty.
3 You cheated in the exam.
4 I want to get my hair cut like yours.
5 We won't be late.
6 You look as if you've lost weight.
7 I'm going to reduce your salary.
8 It's a long time since I've eaten such delicious food.

4

2 (that) you'd been there / to New Orleans.
3 (that) you didn't want one / an ice cream.
4 (that) the room would cost £120.
5 (that) Mr Cooper / he'd be free at three o'clock.
6 (that) you'd posted it / the letter to Sachs & Co.
7 (that) the food at the Pizza Parlour is / was terrible.
8 (that) I had / I'd got / I've got plenty of time to get to the airport.

5a

2 I asked the police officer what the time was.
3 The lawyer asked the witness if she had ever seen the man before.
4 My grandma asked me why I didn't visit her more often.
5 Luc asked Vanessa whether she'd like to go out for dinner.
6 They asked us whether we thought we were ready for the challenge.

7 The teacher asked Tony who the president of Australia was.
8 The waiter asked us whether we'd like to see the dessert menu.

5b

2 What's the time?
3 Have you ever seen the man before?
4 Why don't you visit me more often?
5 Would you like to go out for dinner?
6 Do you think you're ready for the challenge?
7 Who is the president of Australia?
8 Would you like to see the dessert menu?

6

2 b	3 b	4 a	5 a
6 b	7 a	8 b	

7

2 denied	4 blamed	5 warned
7 assured	10 agreed / decided	

8

2 She refused to pay.
3 She denied breaking the photocopier.
4 She complained that the food was undercooked. / She complained about the food.
5 She warned Pat that the roads were very slippery. / She warned Pat to be careful because the roads were very slippery. / She warned pat about the slippery roads.
6 She threatened to call the police (if they didn't turn the noise down).
7 He offered to have a look at my/our/their TV.
8 She blamed Geoff for the misunderstanding.

9

2 Is that Frank? You're on *Eastern Suburbs Talk* **Radio** – what's your question for the team?
3 I've never met Stephanie, but Robert's always spoken very **well** of her.
4 What's worrying you, Todd? Come on, you're not usually afraid to speak your **mind**.
5 Are you and Paula on speaking **terms** again yet?
6 I bought her some flowers as a way of saying sorry. After all, '**Actions** speak louder than words,' as they say.
7 Jon certainly knows what he's talking **about** when it comes to choosing a new laptop.
8 You'll have to speak **up** when you're giving your presentation – it's a very big room.
9 I'm sorry to talk **shop** at the weekend, but I need to ask you about the Freeman report.
10 At 9.30 we're showing ITC's new talk **show**, hosted by comedian Dean Skinner.
11 I wasn't talking **to** myself, I was using the earpiece on my mobile phone – look!
12 The national lottery scandal is a real talking **point** all over the country at the moment.
13 Do we have to go to the party? You know I hate making **small** talk with Annie and Jeff's friends.

10a

2

10b

1 F	2 F	3 T	4 F	5 T	6 T

11a

2 According to the article
3 Apparently,
4 I was surprised to find that
5 The main point that comes out of it is
6 I'd be interested to hear what you think.

UNIT 11

1a

2 What would you do if you became a world leader?
3 What part of your body would you change if you could?
4 If you had to live on a desert island, what would you take with you?
5 What would you rescue from your home if it was on fire?
6 If you could change places with anyone, who would you choose?
7 What would you study if you went back to school?
8 What would you do if you only had four weeks to live?

1b

a 2; I'd try to make the gap between rich and poor narrower.
b 5; I'd save as many of my books as I **could**.
c 8; I'd eat and drink anything I **wanted**!
d 1; If my children **were** a bit older, I'd take them on a world tour.
e 4; I think I'd take a camera, so I **could** record the experience.
f 3; My hands – **I'd love** to have slim, elegant fingers.
g 7; **I'd learn** Italian, so I could read all those wonderful, old Italian recipe books.
h 6; If it **was/were** just for a day, I'd choose a supermodel!

2

2 If only I could drive.
3 I wish Sally would speak up. I can hardly hear her.
4 If only we were still on holiday.
5 If only I didn't get so nervous before exams.
6 I wish you would be quiet and listen to me.

3

2 It's time we went home.
3 It's time the children were in bed.
4 It's time Jo realised that money doesn't grow on trees.
5 It's time you learnt/learned to cook for yourself!
6 It's time we did more to protect our environment.

4a

/ɪ/ ex*ample*	/ɔː/ m*ore*	/ʊə/ p*ure*	/iː/ m*e*
eruption surface	dinosaur	fuel	catastrophe
/ə/ *teacher*	/eɪ/ *say*	/ɒ/ h*ot*	/ɪə/ *area*
temperature ocean	radioactive	volcanic	nuclear
/ɔɪ/ v*oid*	/əʊ/ n*o*	/aɪ/ s*ilent*	
asteroid	solar volcano	scientific dioxide	

5a

1 turn   2 disappeared, prevent   3 causes, contribute
4 reflect, impact   5 combat, affects

5b

2 e   3 a   4 b   5 c

6a

1 F   2 T   3 T   4 F   5 F

6b

1 chocolate   2 very small flakes of skin
3 exercising in the evening   4 a pound of coffee
5 viruses

6c

1 Because our muscles are warmer and we are more flexible.
2 A dog – cats are twice as likely to cause allergic reactions.
3 Yes.
4 They both contain antioxidants, which can protect against cholesterol and cancer.
5 Make a second brew.

7

2 b   3 b   4 a   5 b   6 a   7 a   8 b

8

1 have been
2 hadn't told
3 hadn't woken, have missed
4 hadn't mentioned, wouldn't have noticed
5 hadn't told, have asked, have offered
6 had listened, have got
7 'd known, would (you) have gone, 'd looked

9

1b would still be   2a wouldn't be
2b wouldn't have collapsed   3a wouldn't have
3b would have saved   4a would have passed
4b would have   5a wouldn't have lost
5b wouldn't be retyping

10

2 lifeguard   3 life-threatening   4 life difficult
5 It was the chance of a lifetime!   6 life-like   7 life sentence
8 lifelong

11b

2 Just over half   3 On the whole,   4 A quarter
5 Three out of five   6 The vast majority

12a

1 C   2 A   3 D   4 B

12b

In favour: three arguments   Against: three arguments

12c

2 Secondly   3 For example   4 Furthermore/Also
5 However   6 remember   7 Another argument is that
8 Also/Furthermore   9 In conclusion   10 in my opinion

UNIT 12

1a

2 b   3 f   4 a   5 i   6 h
7 e   8 c   9 g

1b

2 draw huge crowds   3 overnight sensation
4 splashed (across the) newspapers   5 ill-equipped (to) deal with
6 reputation   7 diva   8 make (a) comeback
9 media spotlight

2a

1 Know your audience   2 Choose the right spark
3 Emphasise the spark   4 Create a meme
5 Check for copycats

Answer key

2b

1 T   2 F (Even if you want it to have universal appeal, you still need to consider your audience.)   3 F (It can have limited appeal.)
4 T   5 F (You need to promote it – 'turn up the volume' here refers metaphorically to talking about it a lot.)   6 T

2c

1 c   2 e   3 a   4 d   5 b

3

2 think	3 not to see	4 to answer
5 to thank	6 to believe	7 borrow, to be
8 to read	9 to eat	10 to suggest
11 go	12 not to come	13 to find
14 to tell, not to offer		

4

2 to create	3 to provide / provide	4 to get
5 be sending	6 to play	7 helping
8 make / to make	9 introducing	10 to stop

5

2 In the summer you should avoid going out in the midday sun.
3 Al denied eating the rest of the chocolates.
4 I'm getting used to driving an automatic car.
5 I lost weight by doing lots of exercise and counting calories.
6 Tickets sell out quickly, so it's worth phoning the box office to check first.
7 I'm sorry, madam, I'm having trouble finding your details on the computer.
8 If you don't mind waiting, I can get you a table next to the window.
9 Are you considering applying for the job in Madrid?
10 One of the best things about the summer is being able to eat outside.
11 Are you looking forward to seeing all your old school friends tomorrow?
12 I miss having the beach opposite my apartment.

6

2 to spend	3 to leave	4 trying
5 leaving	6 playing	7 to trust
8 meeting	9 get	10 to meet
11 to find out	12 Cheating	

7a

2 to be locked up	3 not being woken up	5 not being
7 seems to be coming	8 I'd like to have learnt	

8a

1 to give	2 being chased, to leave
3 to show	4 to tip
5 to have changed	6 to do
7 be included	8 get
9 be	10 suggesting, be included

8b

b 10	c 4	d 2	e 1
f 8	g 3	h 9	i 6

9a

2 You should <u>focus</u> on <u>winning</u> the <u>race</u>.
3 We'd <u>like</u> to have <u>known</u> about it <u>sooner</u>.
4 I <u>hate</u> being <u>told</u> what to <u>do</u>.
5 You <u>promised</u> <u>not</u> to be <u>late</u>.
6 I <u>want</u> to be <u>lying</u> on a <u>beach</u> right now.

10a

A What would you like to be famous for?
B Do celebrities have the right to a private life?

10b

2 mind   3 seems   4 the   5 stressful   6 being

Pearson Education Limited
Edinburgh Gate
Harlow
Essex CM20 2JE
England
and Associated Companies throughout the world.

www.pearsonelt.com

First published 2013
Eight impression 2019

ISBN: 978-1-4479-0677-3

Set in 10.5pt Bliss Light
Printed in L.E.G.O. S.p.A., Italy

Photo acknowledgements
*The publisher would like to thank the following for their kind permission
to reproduce their photographs:*

(Key: b-bottom; c-centre; l-left; r-right; t-top)

akg-images Ltd: Schütze / Rodemann 73br; **Alamy Images:** Cultura
Creative 62l, OJO Images Ltd 30; **Corbis:** DoD 65br, Gabriela Hasbun /
Aurora Photos 42tl, STR / epa 42br; **Digital Vision:** 65t; **Fotolia.
com:** Africa Studio 20cr, Peter Atkins 59, bertys30 44t (Racers), Buriy
44b (Horizon), Zdenka Darula 64, Warren Goldswain 67b, illustrez-
vous 44c (Nutty), jaymast 14cr, Alexey Klementiev 71, lassedesignen
65c (Globe), Micky75 66, milosluz 20bl, mimagephotos 22, nyul 5,
Bombaert Patrick 44t (Grippers), pizuttipics 44b (Genesis), Jonathan
Stutz 49, tycoon101 68, Serghei Velusceac 44c (Nut and Choc); **Getty
Images:** 42cr, Jupiterimages 39; **Pearson Education Ltd:** 18b; **Press
Association Images:** Bernd Weissbrod / DPA 42bl, Doug Peters /
EMPICS Entertainment 73tl; **Rex Features:** Broadimage 9, Moviestore
Collection 12tr, 12cl, Philip Reeve 19, Snap Stills 35; **Shutterstock.
com:** Africa Studio 67t, bluehand 65c (Plankton), Norman Chan
20bc, conrado 55br, Elena Elisseeva 6t, FocusDzign 18t, Goodluz
57, jl661227 65bl, Robert Kneschke 6b, Lucky Business 54, Carsten
Medom Madsen 74, Minerva Studio 14tl; **SuperStock:** Martin Benik /
Westend61 27, PhotoAlto 40

Cover images: *Front:* **Fotolia.com:** Beboy

All other images © Pearson Education

Every effort has been made to trace the copyright holders and we
apologise in advance for any unintentional omissions. We would be
pleased to insert the appropriate acknowledgement in any subsequent
edition of this publication.

Illustrated by Colin Brown, Nicky Dupays, Conny Jude, Tim Kahane,
Sam Thompson (Eikon) and Theresa Tibbetts (Beehive Illustration).